APOCALYPSE RISING

DWAIN MILLER

Published by

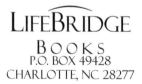

LifeBridge
B O O K S
P.O. BOX 49428
CHARLOTTE, NC 28277

DEDICATION

This book is dedicated to Jerry Miller. He is a servant of the Lord who has faithfully preached the Word of God for almost six decades!

He has taught me more than I could ever articulate. He is a masterful Preacher, Pastor, Husband, Man of God, and most importantly, my DAD!

He is my Hero!
He is my BEST FRIEND!

Contents

FOREWORD

For the first time in print, prophetic and Jewish roots expert, Dr. Dwain Miller reveals the coming Antichrist and the False Prophet.

With Biblical clarity and historical insight Dr. Miller unveils the dark paths from Rome and the Islamic world to the apocalypse. He debunks the idea that the end time leader will arise from Europe and gives decisive proof of Antichrist's Islamic roots. A revived Ottoman Empire will be led by an Islamic son of Satan.

Amazingly, Dr. Miller sees the final world religious leader ascending out of Rome, leading an unholy amalgamation of apostate Christians joined with Islam and other world religions in a vast unified and unholy faith.

As terrifying as these prospects seem, Dr. Miller lifts up the blessed hope of Christ's coming for the church prior to the judgements of the Great Tribulation.

This book resonates with tradition-shattering truth while also throbbing with heartfelt hope. This is a must-have for every believer who desires to understand and live with wisdom in these last days.

You will want to share the God given revelation in this volume with everyone you know.

Thank you Dr. Miller for this fearless and timely book.

> – *Dr. Ron Phillips*
> *Pastor's Study*
> *Abbas House*
> *Chattanooga , Tennessee*

INTRODUCTION

It was a hot summer night in the foothills of the Ozark Mountains and the people of the Providence Baptist Church had gathered for summer revival.

The little country church was different shades of tan and brown as its exterior was made from the native stone of that region. The small building was surrounded by an aged cemetery filled with old oak trees that seemed to reach to the heavens. At least that's how they appeared to a nine-year-old boy.

The church had really grown in the first year of my father's tenure there as pastor. We had achieved a great luxury—indoor toilets. It sure was nice to no longer have to fight red wasps to use the outhouse!

Reflecting back to that night, I remember the church was packed. The small overflow rooms on the side and back of the sanctuary that served as Sunday school rooms, had their accordion style doors slid all the way open so that we could accommodate the overflow crowd.

Our evangelist, a lifelong friend of my father's, Dr. Bobby Clark, stood at the pulpit that night and in his own style and fashion delivered a message on the rapture of the church. As was his custom, he preached well over an hour and not missing one word or pausing to take much of a breath, the spittle flew from his mouth as he eloquently painted the picture of Christ's returning at the shout and sound of a trumpet.

As he described the dead in Christ bodies bursting forth from the grave, he pointed toward the cemetery on the outside of the building. He then went on to tell how those who were alive in Christ would be taken from the earth faster than one could blink their eye.

As a young boy, it was typically my custom to find a friend or two to sit with in church. This afforded me the opportunity to amuse myself with drawing or writing notes and passing them around to my buddies. However, on this night, while I was sitting with a friend near the back left side of the building, we were all unusually paying attention to Dr. Clark with peaked interest.

"Brother Bobby," as we affectionately called

him, was preaching with the fiery passion of the old time hell fire and damnation Baptist delivery. He was so loud that no sound system was required, and even your ears would reverberate with the intensity of his voice. Sweating through his suit and with beads of perspiration pouring from his balding head, he would pause only to take the white handkerchief from his back pocket and wipe the moisture from his brow, the spit from his lips, and then continue on with fiery fervor.

That night, in the summer of 1976, my life was forever changed. For when Brother Bobby gave the altar call and described the great judgment that would come to those who missed the rapture, I thought my heart would beat out of my chest. Then, one of my buddies, sitting next to the aisle, walked out and went down front to my awaiting father. I saw him get down on his knees beside my dad and give his heart to Jesus Christ as Lord and Savior! The invitation went on and on! People filled the altar.

With white knuckles gripping the back of the pew, and my heart feeling like it would explode, I held on for what seemed to be an hour!

Soon, all those who had "gotten saved," as we called it, were lined up across the front and officially received as candidates for Baptism. I thought the conviction I was under would go away. But, it did not. All I could imagine was that Jesus would return in the clouds and take everyone in my family but me—and there I would be, left behind to go through all the horrific events that Brother Bobby had just preached about.

I approached my father by the door of the church after the building had almost emptied. I pulled on his suit coat to get his attention. He stands six feet, two inches tall. He is a man with wide shoulders, a commanding voice and a very intimidating presence. But, that evening when I told him I needed to "get saved," his voice quivered and a tear welled up in his eyes as we went into the nursery of the church.

It was there on our knees that my father opened his Bible and led me through the Roman Road of Salvation. I prayed and asked Jesus to forgive my sin and be my Lord. He graciously did!

It was on that summer night my love for Bible Prophecy was birthed. I studied it at every opportunity. As a teenager of 16, the Lord began calling me into the ministry. At 18, I surrendered to His will. Among the first sermons that I ever preached, Bible Prophecy was front and center.

Dr. Bobby Clark and my father, Jerry Miller, have taught me more than almost anyone else. Brother Bobby passed away a couple of years ago. I truly miss our two hour phone conversations concerning the Middle-East and all that is rounding into shape concerning the end times.

My Dad, however is still a pastor and preaching stronger than ever at the age of 76. As I write this he has been faithfully delivering the Word of God for 56 years! He and I still have occasion to sit and discuss world events and how the things that he preached 40 years ago are coming to pass right before our very eyes.

This book is a compilation and an overview of current events and how they meld into the Scriptures. I truly believe that we are at the door of the Lord's return. I owe this knowledge to these men of God who have mentored my life.

– Dr. Dwain Miller

PART ONE

THE FALSE PROPHET

CHAPTER 1

THE APOSTATE CHURCH

To say that the world today is imploding is an understatement.

My heart cries out for the Christians in the Middle East. For the first time in history, believers in Christ have been run from their homes in Mosul, Iraq, by ISIS, the so-called Islamic State. Some of the oldest Christian families, dating back to the times of Jesus—and speaking the same Aramaic language He spoke—were threatened to either convert or be brutally killed. Many fled, but untold thousands have been savagely murdered.

In February, 2015, I shuddered as I watched the video of ISIS beheading 21 Coptic Christians from Egypt who were working in Lybia. At the edge of the Mediterranean Sea, dressed in orange jumpsuits with their hands cuffed behind them, a masked English-speaking jahadi announced, "The sea you have hidden Sheikh Osama bin Ladin's body in, we swear to Allah, we will mix with your blood."

Then, as if on cue, all of the victims were pushed down to the ground and beheaded. Their bodies were thrown into the blood-stained water.

Terror knows no boundaries. It happens at the Boston marathon, in an Australian coffee shop, and at a Jewish grocery store in Paris.

WHO ARE OUR ENEMIES?

What are we to think when Russia walks into Crimea and literally steals the land from the sovereign nation of Ukraine? The world seems to shrug its shoulders and allows bullies to continue their wicked ways!

On July 17, 2014, Malaysia Airlines Flight 17 was en route from Amsterdam to Kuala Lumpur. Flying over an area of Ukraine controlled by pro-Russian separatists, the Boeing 777 with 283 passengers and 15 crew on board, was suddenly shot down by a missile. There were no survivors.

Six days later, CNN reported, "Vitaly Nayda,

Ukraine's director of informational security, told CNN the person who shot down the flight was 'absolutely' a Russian. A Russian-trained, well-equipped, well-educated officer...pushed that button deliberately," he said. Nayda added, "We taped conversations between a Russian officer and his office in Moscow. We know for sure that several minutes before the missile was launched, there was a report to a Russian officer that the plane was coming."

Again, no one was held accountable and we carry on, acting as if our enemies are our friends.

It boggles the mind that the U.S. government has given the nation of Iran 14 billion of our taxpayer dollars to entice them to negotiate over their building of a nuclear weapon. This is insanity! The same is true for handing Hamas $14 million when they are dedicated to wiping Israel off the map.

Personally, I believe that neither the government nor the church can negotiate with a demon.

Departing from the Faith

Without question, we are living in the last days.

Jesus declared, *"You will hear of wars and rumors of wars...For nation will rise against nation, and kingdom against kingdom. And there will be famines, pestilences, and earthquakes in various places...and you will be hated by all nations for My name's sake"* (Matthew 24: 6-7,9).

In this book I am shining a spotlight on another passage from God's Word—and walking you through events that are quickly leading to the apocalypse that is rising before our very eyes.

It is written in 1 Timothy 4:1-2, *"Now the Spirit expressly says that in latter times some will depart from the faith, giving heed to deceiving spirits and doctrines of demons, speaking lies in hypocrisy, having their own conscience seared with a hot iron..."*

When the Bible proclaims that in the final days many will *"depart from the faith,"* the only conclusion I can draw is that you have to be *in* the faith in order to depart from it. In other words, many will *apostate* themselves.

At this very moment, there is an apostate church that is surging. Men and women who claim to know and profess Jesus Christ are now walking away from the truth, believing a lie. You can't trust what they are saying and doing because they have ulterior, ungodly motives.

A CHARGE TO KEEP

As a minister of the Gospel, there is only one way I can respond to the climactic events that are unfolding before my eyes. I must be accountable to the mandate given by Paul the Apostle:

I charge you therefore before God and the Lord Jesus Christ, who will judge the living and the dead at His appearing and His kingdom: Preach the word!

Be ready in season and out of season. Convince, rebuke, exhort, with all longsuffering and teaching. For the time will come when they will not endure sound doctrine, but according to their own desires, because they have itching ears, they will heap up for themselves teachers; and they will turn their ears away from the truth, and be turned aside to fables.

But you be watchful in all things, endure afflictions, do the work of an evangelist, fulfill your ministry (2 Timothy 4:1-5).

21

Let me say, as humbly and as sincerely as I can, that the days when preachers would stand in pulpits, declare the truth, and be applauded for their bold declarations are fast becoming distant memories. In the here and now when ministers, such as myself stand firmly on the Word of God, we are the targets of persecution, testing, and affliction—not just from the secular media, but from within the church itself!

In the hours ahead, it's certainly not going to be popular or glamorous to herald the unadulterated message of Christ. This is why Paul warned Timothy against preaching a watered-down, feel-good Gospel.

What are we to do with God's Word? Exactly what I am sharing with you in this book—and allow the facts to speak for themselves.

A BEAST WITH AUTHORITY

According to Scripture, there is an ominous figure who will emerge from the nations. John, in the revelation given to him by God, says: *"Then I saw another beast coming out of the earth, and he had two horns like a lamb and spoke like a dragon"* (Revelation 13:11).

The first beast is the Antichrist, who we will deal with in Part Two of this book, but this second beast, the false prophet, ascends out of the nations of the earth with leadership and political authority.

He is a religious leader, and the two horns mentioned symbolize the two branches of authority he possesses:

1. Great religious and spiritual influence because of his position.
2. Great political authority because of wealth and prestige.

In appearance, this false prophet is like a lamb —seeming harmless and extremely accessible and approachable. But he speaks with the mouth of Satan, the dragon.

The Bible tells us:

He exercises all the authority of the first beast (the Antichrist) in his presence, and causes the earth and those who dwell in it to worship the first beast, whose deadly wound was healed.

He performs great signs, so that he even makes fire come down from heaven on the earth in the sight of men. And he deceives those who dwell on the earth by those signs which he was granted to do in the sight of the beast, telling those who dwell on the earth to make an image to the beast who was wounded by the sword and lived" (verses 12-15).

In addition, we learn that he *"causes all, both small and great, rich and poor, free and slave, to receive a mark on their right hand or on their foreheads, and that no one may buy or sell except one who has the mark or the name of the beast, or the number of his name. Here is wisdom. Let him who has understanding calculate the number of the beast [the Antichrist], for it is the number of a man: His number is 666"* (verses 16-18).

WEALTH AND INFLUENCE

Allow me to place this in a time line.

At the midway point of the tribulation, there is a seven year period called "Daniel's 70th Week" (see Daniel 9).

The first three and a half years are going to resemble what things look like right now. But half way into that period, for the last 42 months, comes what is called The Great Tribulation.

This is when the Antichrist will receive a wound in his head. As we will detail later, I believe it is a political wound.

It is also when the false prophet will be elevated into prominence. This renowned religious leader with unparalleled influence and wealth will politically, socially, economically, and spiritually come to the defense of this world figure (the Antichrist) and will re-establish him in the earth as a major force. With signs, wonders, and miracles, the false prophet will cause mankind to worship the Antichrist.

THE DECEIVER

I am a pastor who believes that miracles still happen today; they did not cease with Christ and the apostles.

That being said, we cannot believe everything that occurs under the banner of Christianity. There have always been aberrations and unexplainable phenomenon—and these will increase. As Jesus warned, *"False christs and false prophets will rise and show great signs and wonders to deceive, if possible, even the elect"* (Matthew 24:24).

These impostors will abound in growing numbers, so you need to pray for discernment to separate truth from error. The test I recommend is to ask yourself:

- Was Jesus glorified?
- Were people brought to Christ?
- Were the sick healed?
- Were the bound delivered?

If man is at the forefront instead of God's Son, you'd better run! Otherwise you will be dealing with the spirit of the Antichrist loosed in the earth.

POWER OVER COMMERCE

Back to the time line, the false prophet will set up an image of the Antichrist in the rebuilt temple in Jerusalem and command that all worship there. As we read in 2 Thessalonians 2:3-4: *"Let no one deceive you by any means; for that Day will not come unless the falling away comes first, and the man of sin is revealed, the son of perdition, who opposes and exalts himself above all that is called God or that is worshiped, so that he sits as God in the temple of God, showing himself that he is God."*

In order to manipulate mankind to bow before the Antichrist, the false prophet will have power over commerce. You will not be able to buy, sell, eat, drink, or live unless you receive the mark of the beast. We will dig deeper into this as we move along.

The false prophet, in my opinion, based on Revelation 17, is the leader of the harlot church. You can make your own conclusion as to who you think that church is.

According to Scripture, in John's revelation, one of the seven angels came to him, saying, *"Come,*

I will show you the judgment of the great harlot who sits on many waters, with whom the kings of the earth committed fornication, and the inhabitants of the earth were made drunk with the wine of her fornication" (Revelation 17:1-2).

The *"many waters"* is interpreted later in this same chapter as being *"peoples, multitudes, nations, and tongues"* (verse 15). In other words, this church is worldwide, influencing men and women everywhere.

For the sake of the wealth that this religious force possesses, kings, nations, and national leaders commit spiritual fornication, selling their souls to its cause and buying her doctrine. Why? Because being connected to this church can position them to have enormous success in the kingdom of the Antichrist.

THE BLOOD OF SAINTS

Next, John writes, the angel *"carried me away in the Spirit into the wilderness. And I saw a woman sitting on a scarlet beast..."* (Revelation 17:3). Here we have the marriage between religion and politics—uniting the false prophet, the great harlot church, and the Antichrist (who is the beast carrying this religious system).

We learn that *"this beast was full of names of blasphemy, having seven heads and ten horns. The woman was arrayed in purple and scarlet, and adorned with gold and precious stones and pearls, having in her hand a golden cup full of abominations and the filthiness of her fornication. And on her forehead a name was written: MYSTERY, BABYLON THE GREAT, THE MOTHER OF HARLOTS AND OF THE ABOMINATIONS OF THE EARTH. I saw the woman, drunk with the blood of the saints"* (verses 3-6).

This woman/church was extremely wealthy and extravagant in her worship. But the world commits immorality with her by drinking from the golden cup and joining in covenant with her shame.

It's amazing but true that this church has actually killed Christians and has, for practically her entire existence, been noted for having martyred those who disagreed with her.

Let me challenge you to study church history, especially in the dark ages, when the Bible was taken out of every person's hands and only the priests of this system were allowed to read and preach the Word of God.

It is a sad story that millions of our Methodist, Baptist, Lutheran, and other Protestant ancestors were slaughtered by this church for resisting her doctrine.

The word "Protestant," itself, derives from the *protests* over the stranglehold this dominant entity had on religion.

SEVEN HILLS AND TEN NATIONS

Who is this harlot who has *"seven heads and ten horns"* (Revelation 17:3)? It was revealed to John, *"The seven heads are seven mountains [or a city of seven hills] on which the woman sits"* (verse 9).

And what about the *"ten horns"*? As we will learn, in the middle of the tribulation, she controls a ten-nation federation of the Middle East, which I will be naming.

Growing up, you probably heard as I did that there would come a "one world government" and a "one world economic system." This is not prophesied in the Bible.

Instead, there is a Middle Eastern-Western arrangement of buying, selling, and commerce that the Antichrist will control. China and Asia will not be included in this alliance.

I have concluded that the reason China and Asia fight in the battle of Armageddon is because their economy will have crashed. Why? Because the Antichrist has driven them into the ground and he is controlling the commerce of Europe, the Middle East, Africa, and the West. The Chinese will not arrive with 200,000 soldiers simply to fight the Jews. Their troops will be sent to battle the Antichrist—because if they fail to take over, their economic power will be totally vanquished.

BUYING INTO THE LIE

The immoral fornication between politics and the church, spoken of in Revelation 17, is a description of what could happen in America.

I believe this is taking place in evangelical churches today who are buying this lie from the false church system. The handwriting is on the wall. If present trends continue, people in America can and will become so desperate economically that they will sell their soul to *anything* if it will feed them, clothe them, and pay their bills.

Ministries are vulnerable too. They can become so large, powerful, and self-absorbed that they will do whatever it takes for more recognition, more power, more members, more partners, more money. This thing called "success in ministry" can be extremely dangerous.

According to God's Word, the greatest success you and I can ever have is to become servants of one another.

LOSING OUR WAY

We must wake up! This harlot church and the false prophet from her, has to very elaborately draw in all religious systems in the Middle East to drink from her golden cup. There are three: Islam, Christianity, and Judaism.

Before we examine how this will come about, let me give you an example of how easy it is for churches to lose their way.

Ten or fifteen years ago we didn't understand

what is called the "church growth movement." But many congregations have been touched by it—including Baptists, Methodists, Lutherans, Assemblies of God, evangelicals and charismatics.

This movement emerged with a pure motive, but ultimately, success began to be measured by "nickels and noses." So leaders started changing their message to attract more nickels and preach to more noses.

Sadly, the Gospel in America has become diluted until it is almost unrecognizable. Recently, a megachurch pastor was interviewed on a national talk show and was asked, "Will a homosexual go to heaven?"

He answered, "Well, I'm not sure, but as for me..."

God doesn't give a rip what you and I believe about the subject. His Word clearly addresses the issue (among so many others) and that's the final answer.

But for the sake of building churches we want to be "inclusive" and not risk upsetting the social applecart. "Let's just all get along and love each other."

This is the danger that is sucking the American

church into the lie of the false prophet.

Sincere, Yet Blind

Let me give you a prime example.

When a major Baptist pastor justifies his non-confrontational approach to the Gospel by joining hands and praying with Muslims in order to meet the humanitarian needs of children in Africa, this should give us reason for great concern.

I'm all for him sending food to Islamic children who are starving in the Sudan. But in order to do that, I refuse to renounce the fact that Jesus is the way, the truth, and the life.

You can feed the bodies of children, but if they die and go to Hell, you've done no one a favor.

Will a Muslim Imam let you travel with him and tell those hungry boys and girls, "Here is some bread, but let me introduce you to Jesus, who is the Bread of Life"?

Will he let you share with them, "You may not have everything in this life, but let me tell you how to live forever"?

There are countless leaders in evangelical and charismatic churches who are sincere, yet seem completely blind. My heart grieves for them—and the people to whom they are ministering.

They are oblivious to the fact that there is coming a marriage between Judaism, Christianity, and Islam. It will not only take place, but the false prophet will perform the ceremony!

You may protest, "That's impossible!"

Well, hold on. As they say, "It's coming to a theater near you!"

CHAPTER 2

THE FINAL POPE?

In Part Two of this book you will learn how the Antichrist will be a Muslim and will emerge from a system that revived Rome. First, let's examine some vital background.

The ancient Roman empire was standing on two legs, east and west. The east branch was the Greek Orthodox church and the west branch the Roman Catholic church. Baptists and Pentecostals were born out of the eastern branch. That's why at baptism we immerse believers in water rather than sprinkle them.

During the 15th century, the Ottoman Empire invaded Turkey and overthrew Christianity. In Constantinople (now Istanbul), the largest Greek Orthodox church, the Hagai Sophia, was turned into an Islamic mosque—and remains under Muslim control to this very day.

The Antichrist and his system, religion, and

government will rise out of the eastern branch of a revived Roman empire, and the false prophet will surface from the western branch, which is Rome. Both Istanbul and Rome boast the title, "The City of Seven Hills"—which the Bible says both beasts will come out of.

Now let's turn our attention to Jerusalem. The world's three dominating religions lay claim to Mount Moriah:

- Judaism says this is the site where Abraham offered Isaac on the altar.
- Christianity teaches that it is where Jesus was crucified, buried, and rose again.
- Islam maintains that their founder, Mohammed, visited there and had an encounter with Allah.

To many it may seem impossible, but I believe the false prophet will be hailed as a genius at bringing the three religions together under the guise of saying, "Let's unite. We are all praying to the same God."

Just as my study of prophecy has led me to believe that the Antichrist will be a Muslim, I also am convinced that a pope will be the false prophet.

You may exclaim, "That's quite a bold statement"—and it is.

Before going into details, let me make it clear that I love people of the Catholic faith and personally know many who have given their hearts to Christ and have a personal relationship with God's Son. What I am about to share with you has nothing to do with individuals who attend mass and are members of the Roman church. However, there is a body of evidence that lines up with both Scripture and prophecy that leads to the startling conclusion that a pontiff will be the false prophet described in Revelation.

SAINT MALACHY'S VISION

In 1139, archbishop Malachy O'Morgair from the city of Armagh, Ireland, was summoned by Pope Innocent II to travel to Rome for an official visit. While there, he experienced a vision of future popes, which he recorded as a sequence of cryptic phrases. This manuscript was then deposited in the Vatican Secret Archives and forgotten about until its rediscovery in 1556, just before a papal conclave ongoing at the time. The first known publication of the prophecy was in a 1595 volume by Arnold de Wion entitled *Lignum Vitae* (Tree of Life).

The vision, which Malachy said was given to him by the Holy Spirit, listed the characteristics of 112 future popes, starting with Celestine the Second whose papacy was in 1143-1144.

Father Malachy was so accurate in his prophecies, and there were so many miracles that took place in his ministry, that the Catholic church gave him the coveted title, "Saint Malachy."

The landmark book on this subject is *Petrus Romanus* by Thomas Horn and Cris Putnam and I am indebted to them for many of the facts I am sharing and highly recommend that you read this eye-opening volume.

In the original vision, God revealed to Malachy that the 112th pope would be the last pontiff and that the end of time and life on earth as we know it would draw to a close.

Here is why this prophecy is so significant. Pope Francis, the current papal leader, is the 112th pope.

It is believed by many Catholic bishops prophets, and scholars of years gone by that the final pope would reign as the nations gathered for the Battle of Armageddon.

Specifically, Saint Malachy wrote that the 112th pope would be named Petrus Romanus, or Peter the Roman.

In the translations of Malachy's description of future popes, here is what he said concerning the final pontiff, "Peter the Roman will pasture his sheep in many tribulations, and when things are finished, the city of seven hills [i.e. Rome] will be destroyed, and the dreadful judge will judge his people. The End."

QUESTIONING HIS NAME

When Pope Benedict XVI suddenly resigned in 2013 and Pope Francis ascended to the papal throne and chose the name Francis, after Saint Francis of Assisi, there were many who shook their heads and murmured, "See, Saint Malachy was wrong. He missed it because he didn't choose the name Peter."

Others, however, believed the name "Peter" is

irrelevant, because *all* popes think of themselves as Peter—since they believe Peter was the first pope. But if the prophecy revealed that the last pope would be "Petrus Romanus," this meant he had to be Italian.

Taking a close look at Pope Francis, however, we find that even though he was born in Argentina, his parents were Italian immigrants—so he is full-blooded Italian.

In addition, before Saint Francis of Assisi (1181-1228) took his title, his birth name was Giovani di Petro Bernardone. So the current Pope Francis chose what he was to be called after a previous saint of the Catholic church who had Peter in his name.

The renown prophecy teacher Jack Van Impe points out that Pope John Paul II and Pope Benedict believed in Saint Malachy's prophecies and did all they could to make sure that the pope who followed them would be theologically conservative. These men were well aware that in the end times there would come a great apostacy of cardinals, bishops, and clergy of the Catholic church.

Dr. Van Impe states that John Paul II was so convinced that the 112th pope would be the last that he tried to divert the prophecy by appointing 185 out of 190 cardinals during his reign. In the process he chose conservative cardinals, believing that if he could fill the Vatican leadership with such men they would not follow after the liberal teachings of a pope who might attempt to mislead the church.

LIGHTNING STRUCK!

In my opinion, and that of many of my Catholic friends, Pope Benedict XVI was the most conservative papal leader in our lifetime.

He believed in salvation by grace through faith, just as evangelicals do. He was clear in his teachings that a man or woman could only be saved through the blood of Jesus.

If you take the time to read some of Benedict's writings and doctrines you will find that he was firm in the belief of the second coming of Christ. For example (in his Catechism, point 840), he states that "one awaits the return of the Messiah who died and rose from the dead and is recognized as Lord and Son of God." And he prayed in point 2817, "'Maranatha,' the cry of the Spirit and the Bride: 'Come, Lord Jesus'...Indeed, as soon as possible, Lord, may Your kingdom come." (See www.vatican.va/archives).

Then suddenly, on Monday, February, 11, 2013, Pope Benedict XVI surprised the church and the world by announcing his impending resignation. In the history of the church, no pope had left while still in office in the previous 598 years, which sparked plenty of rumors and speculation.

It's amazing but true that the day he resigned, lightning struck Saint Peter's Basillica. Within hours, this was a headline on *BBC News, USA Today*, and thousands of media outlets. To many, it appeared that God was expressing His displeasure.

Speaking of the process of choosing a new pope, in Peggy Noonan's column in *The Wall Street Journal*, February 17, 2013, Benedict is quoted as saying at the time he was a Cardinal, "The role of the Holy Spirit in the conclave is to prevent us from electing a pope who will completely destroy the church."

WHO IS THIS MAN?

So here is the question: Is Pope Francis the false prophet of the Book of Revelation? What I am presenting on these pages are facts. It's up to you to process them, pray about it, and make your own decision.

On March 12, 2013, 115 cardinal-electors gathered at the Vatican to elect a new leader of the church. The next day, after the fifth ballot, a puff of white smoke was seen emanating from the chimney of the Sistine Chapel, signaling there had been an election. Bells began pealing and the crowds of the faithful were cheering. They soon learned that a cardinal from South America would lead the Catholic church.

The first impressions of Pope Francis were extremely positive. Because of his servant-like attitude and the way he reached out to the masses, he was described as "a man of the people" and "like a lamb."

During his years in Argentina, he was heralded for how he cared for the poor and disenfranchised —and the compassion he showed for those who were caught up in various lifestyles—even if they didn't necessarily line up with Catholic doctrine.

As was soon obvious, the secular press was fascinated and enthralled with the new Catholic leader. *The Washington Post* ran a story with the headline, "Who Doesn't like Pope Francis?" and *Time* magazine named him "Person of the Year" for 2013.

As we will see, however, there is another side to the story.

CHAPTER 3

PRINCIPLES, NOT PROCLAMATIONS OR PERSONALITIES

Recently, I was ministering in the city of Managua, Nicaragua. Nearly all of the pastors I met with had come out of Catholicism into Spirit-filled churches in Central America. Without exception, these ministers told me, "The reason Pope Francis was chosen was because he is from Argentina—and the church is dying in Latin America."

Being specific, they added, "On Sunday afternoons the Catholics are holding rallies all across our city. This is their attempt to somehow attract people who left their churches for the gospel of the Holy Spirit to return to their fold. They realize that the great revivals of Latin America and the power of the Spirit is something they cannot compete with—and it's draining their membership."

SURPRISING STATEMENTS

I've always been told that if you want to know what is in a man's heart, pay close attention to his words.

Just two months after his papal inauguration, this headline appeared in the *Huffington Post* on May 22, 2013, "Pope Francis Says Atheists Who Do Good Are Redeemed, Not Just Catholics."

The article quoted the surprising words he spoke that week at a mass in Rome: "The Lord has redeemed all of us...'Father, the atheists?' Even the atheists. Everyone...We must meet one another doing good. 'But I don't believe, Father, I am an atheist!' But do good; we will meet one another there."

"Doing good" is a principle that unites humanity, but in terms of salvation and an eternity in heaven, it is the mark of a universalist, not a Bible-believing follower of Christ.

That same fall, Pope Francis let it be known that he believed Christian fundamentalism is a sickness. As reported by Michal Sean Winters, October 18, 2013, in the *Catholic Reporter,* the pontiff said in his homily that week, "It is a serious illness, this of ideological Christians."

Then, on June 25, 2014, the Pope made this audacious statement to a public audience at St. Peter's Square: "No one becomes a Christian by him-or herself...The Christian belongs to a people called the Church and the Church is what makes him or her Christian." Then he added, "There are those who believe they can maintain a personal, direct and immediate relationship with Jesus Christ outside the communion and the mediation of the Church. These are dangerous and harmful temptations" (www.w2.vatican.va).

Why would he say these things? Does he really believe this?

When Pope Francis visited Turkey in the fall of 2014, he called for an end to all forms of religious fundamentalism. In his meeting with Turkish President Erdogan the pope said, "It is essential that all citizens—Muslim, Jewish and Christian— both in the provision and practice of the Law, enjoy the same rights and respect the same duties. They will then find it easier to see each other as brothers and sisters who are traveling the same path, seeking always to reject misunderstandings while promoting cooperation and concord. Freedom of religion and freedom of expression, when truly guaranteed to each person, will help friendship to flourish and thus become an eloquent sign of peace" (westernjournalism.com).

As you can imagine, statements such as these immediately set off alarm bells in the non-Catholic community, but what about the reaction within the Church itself? It didn't take long before serious questions were being raised.

For example, writing in the *Catholic Family News*, October 14, 2014, John Vennari reported on a presentation given by Bishop Bernard Fellay (Superior General of the Society of Saint Pius X) in Kansas City, Missouri.

Bishop Fellay's remarks centered on *The Third Secret of Fatima* (a 900-year-old prophecy) and its reference to the Apocalypse and the coming of Antichrist. Bishop Fellay noted that Pope Pius X said at the beginning of his pontificate that the "son of perdition" may already be on the earth. He also noted that the original prayer to Saint Michael of Pope Leo XIII mentions that Satan aims to establish his seat in Rome.

After reviewing the present condition of Catholicism, Bishop Fellay stated, "The situation of the Church is a real disaster. And the present Pope (Francis) is making it 10,000 times worse."

THE JESUITS

Much attention was paid to the fact that Pope Francis is the first Jesuit pontiff in history. So to understand his thinking we need to be aware of the fact that the central principle of the Jesuits is to help the poor—any way possible.

This has led many to conclude that, underlying his compassionate acts, there is a deep-seated "take from the rich and give to those in need" philosophy. To some, this is Marxism.

Under the headline, "Pope Francis's Stinging Critique of Capitalism," *The Washington Post* (November 26, 2013), quoted the pontiff as saying, "Some people continue to defend trickle-down theories which assume that economic growth, encouraged by a free market, will inevitably succeed in bringing about greater justice and inclusiveness in the world. This opinion, which has never been confirmed by the facts, expresses a crude and naïve trust in the goodness of those wielding economic power and in the sacralized workings of the prevailing economic system. Meanwhile, the excluded are still waiting...This imbalance is the result of ideologies which defend the absolute autonomy of the marketplace and financial speculation."

A glance into history reveals the concern within the Catholic church over the Jesuits. For instance, Malachi Martin, an Irish Catholic priest and noted instructor at the Vatican's Pontifical Biblical Institute, resigned from his positions in 1963. Why? Because the Jesuit movement (of which he had been a part) made a secret agreement with Nikita Khrushchev to preach and expand Marxist communism to the nations of the earth.

To me, Marxism is a hypocritical ideology because while it preaches redistribution of wealth, its leaders somehow become among the richest men in the world.

It is absolutely amazing how citizens and nations can be deceived into believing a lie.

The false prophet and the Antichrist will use the

Tribulation to dupe believers—those who claim to have a personal relationship with Jesus. Like the serpent in the Garden, they will approach with clever words and intriguing arguments such as, "How can you turn your heart against the poor, the hungry, and the dying? If you will embrace us, we will feed, clothe, and house you."

Scripture warns about those *"whose god is their belly, and whose glory is their shame—who set their mind on earthly things"* (Philippians 3:19).

The false prophet and the Antichrist will unify the religions of the world through commerce and the redistribution of wealth. The key to globalizing any major movement is by removing individuality.

THE SOCIAL AGENDA

The United States of America was founded on basic principles, as stated in the July 4, 1776, Declaration of Independence: "We hold these truths to be self-evident, that all men are created equal, that they are endowed by their Creator with certain unalienable Rights, that among these are Life, Liberty and the pursuit of Happiness."

These personal rights were granted by God and confirmed by our founding fathers to make it possible that if you are willing to work, you can become anything your heart desires. However, year by year, regulation by regulation, our government is robbing our nation of the fundamental bedrock upon which we were established.

As many have said, "Our government is in rebellion against the very purposes of God Almighty." I'm speaking of Republicans, Democrats, and Independents who are buying and selling the lie of Marxist communism that has been watered down into a clever social agenda—so subtle that millions don't recognize what is taking place.

I firmly believe that if the church had been doing its job the last hundred years we would not have bought into these lies.

It is obvious that Pope Francis is on a campaign to unify the religions—including evangelical American Christians—under the umbrella of Rome.

Let me give you just one glimpse of how this is happening.

IN THE NAME OF UNITY

Through a series of circumstances, Anthony "Tony" Palmer, a Charismatic bishop in the Communion of Evangelical Episcopal Churches in South Africa, traveled to Buenos Aires, Argentina, and met with then Cardinal Jorge Mario Bergoglio. The two began a friendship that blossomed over the years.

The CEEC sees itself as a part of a "convergence" movement, seeking to combine evangelical Christianity with the sacraments and liturgy that is found in Catholicism.

As reported by Austin Ivereigh in the *Boston Globe*, August 7, 2014, "At one point, when Palmer was tired of living on the frontier and wanted to become Catholic, Bergoglio advised him against conversion for the sake of the mission. 'We need to have bridge-builders', the cardinal told him."

Even after Bergoglio became Pope Francis, the bond between Palmer and the pontiff continued. In fact, Tony was invited to visit with the pope at the Vatican in January, 2014. During that meeting he used his iPhone to record an impromptu greeting from the Holy Father to an American Charismatic conference that was to be held the next month in the U.S.

At that major event, attended by leading pastors and television evangelists whose names are household words, Tony Palmer set up the showing of the video (available on YouTube) explaining that the pope "wanted to greet all the non-Roman Catholic brothers and sisters and call us all to put an end to the separation of Catholic Christians and all other Christians. It was his [Pope Francis'] desire to speak to us by video...and to give us a personal call to unity; a unity which he told me was not uniformity but a meeting of diversity. In fact, he said to me 'No one is coming home; we are journeying, we are pilgrimaging towards each other and we will meet in the middle. '"

Then the pope appeared on a large media screen, with the words, "I am here with my brother, my bishop brother, Tony Palmer. We've been friends for years. He told me about your conference...and it's my pleasure to greet you. A greeting both joyful and nostalgic. Joyful because it gives me joy that you have come together to worship Jesus Christ the only Lord, and to pray to the Father and to receive the Holy Spirit. This brings me joy because we can see that God is working all over the world. Nostalgic (yearning) because...we are kind of, permit me to say, separated...Let's give each other a spiritual hug and let God complete the work that He has begun. And this is a miracle; the miracle of unity has begun."

When the presentation was over, this group of pastors stood to their feet, applauding, shouting, and praising God.

What were they celebrating?

WHAT DOES THE BIBLE SAY?

Palmer also made a point of stating that in 1999 the Lutheran and the Catholic church resolved the protest of Martin Luther. A document was signed that the Roman Catholic church would adopt the doctrine of Luther that "salvation is by grace through faith alone."

There is no question in my mind that the pope at that time, John Paul II, certainly believed this. But Palmer went on to conclude that the protest is over; there are no Protestants because we are all

Catholic. The word *Catholic* means universal.

Personally, I am not about to lay down my doctrine for a pope who believes that atheists will go to heaven "if they do good." The Gospel I preach and believe has nothing to do with "works." My Bible tells me, *"For by grace you have been saved through faith, and that not of yourselves; it is the gift of God, not of works, lest anyone should boast"* (Ephesians 2:8-9).

A SINCERE OUTREACH?

On July 28, 2014, Pope Francis, flew by helicopter to the village of Caserta, Italy, where he visited a 350-member Pentecostal church and asked for forgiveness regarding the way the Vatican had treated Pentecostals and evangelicals in the past.

While the press heralded the papal visit, not all welcomed the pope's outreach. As reported in *Christianity Today* (online, July 30, 2014), "Many Italian evangelicals are 'increasingly puzzled' by the positive reaction of evangelicals in the United States (and other countries) to the new pope."

The article continued, "'There is much naiveté and superficiality,' wrote Italian church planter

Leonardo De Chirico in a blog post. 'Some analysis is based on personal impressions or the seemingly evangelical language of the pope, or on truncated bits of information that fall short of taking notice of the complexity of Roman Catholicism.' An overwhelming majority of Italy's evangelical churches and organizations—including leaders for the Italian Evangelical Alliance (IEA), the Federation of Pentecostal Churches, and the Assemblies of God in Italy—agree with De Chirico."

Earlier, they signed a statement that provided "biblical standards to assess the mounting ecumenical pressure coming from the Roman Catholic Church to expand its catholicity at the expense of biblical truth."

I say "Hallelujah" to those who express their incompatibility with their personal beliefs and that of the Catholic church and the pope.

Instead of being caught up by a wave of so-called unity that blurs church lines and dilutes doctrines and beliefs, I invite you to open the pages of God's Word and live by what it teaches. Yes, we can have fellowship with believers of different faiths, but when it comes to doctrine, don't be swayed by personalities, but by the principles found in Scripture.

In regard to Tony Palmer. I believe he was a sincere, dedicated man of God, even though I do not agree with his "one church" doctrine. I say "was" because he tragically passed from this life in a motorcycle accident, July 20, 2014.

CHAPTER 4

IN THE NAME
OF UNITY

There are men and women who have tried to link the potential unity of diverse religious groups to "the spirit of Elijah" (Malachi 4) moving upon the earth in the last days: *"And he will turn the hearts of the fathers to the children, and the hearts of the children to their fathers"* (verse 6).

I believe the "spirit of Elijah" is the end time outpouring of the Holy Spirit—and here is what it does. It rejoins the body of Christ to its Hebrew roots. Let me further explain.

You and I are born of a Son that belonged to a Father, not a mother. Your Father is the God of Abraham, Isaac, and Jacob. Your Father has a Son named Jesus Christ, who came as the seed of Abraham. Through His grace and blood you have been grafted into the promise of Abraham. You are a Gentile and do not become a Jew when you are born again.

But you do have the covenant promise of Abraham through Jesus Christ, and you have the identity in your Father not in a mother.

Regardless of what Rome may teach, the church doesn't birth or save anybody. It is not our mother; the church is the bride of Jesus Christ.

Here is what's so exciting. The outpouring of the spirit of Elijah tears down the middle wall of separation between the Jew and Gentile. This spirit shows the love of the Father on this Gentile bride so unconditionally that it spurs the Jews to jealousy (see Romans 9:10-11).

The Jews see that the bride of Christ is taking on her identity as the bride of the Hebrew groom, and they become envious—which pulls them toward salvation. They begin to call on the name of Yeshua as the Messiah, the King of kings and Lord of lords. Out of this comes a great revival in Israel and in the midst of it, the spirit of Elijah will cause the Jews to rebuild their temple.

Never forget that the message of the One New Man (Ephesians 2:15) calls us to our Father. Our *identity* is in our faith, but also we receive our *inheritance* in Him.

THE COMING "MARK"

Looking to Rome is not the solution for the salvation of man, but we need to be totally aware of its place in biblical prophecy.

The Bible is clear that a major world religious leader will unify the religions of the world and establish an economic and ecumenical system or vehicle for the Antichrist to pose as God and rule the earth.

How could Pope Francis possibly be doing anything that would resemble establishing unity among religions?

On the following pages I want to walk you through a series of events that have to do with the mark of the beast, the push toward unifying major religions, and the role of the false prophet.

In 2014 it was announced that Israel would become the first cashless society.

According to *Israel Today*, May 26, 2014, Israel is making plans to become just that—a cashless society. Its journalist, Yossi Aloni, reported, "A special committee headed by Prime Minister Benjamin Netanyahu's chief of staff, Harel Locker, has recommended a three-phase plan to all but do away with cash transactions in Israel."

On the surface, there seem to be many benefits for governments to move in this direction—controlling black market currency, increased tax collections, etc.

However, if you want to know where this is headed, and how fast, do your own research of the amazing growth of human microchip implants. This is where an integrated circuit device or RFID transponder, encased in silicate glass, is implanted in the body. It contains a unique ID number that can be linked to information stored in an external database, such as personal identification, medical history, medications, and even your banking information.

The acceptance of this is coming faster than most people realize. Journalist Mac Salvo, quoted in *New American*, May 3, 2013, writes, "First, the technologies will need to be generally accepted by society. It'll start with real-time consumer based products like Google Glass. The older generations may reject it, but in a couple of years you can bet that tens of millions of kids, teens and younger adults will be roaming the streets while sporting cool shades, interactive web surfing and the capability to record everything around them and upload it to the internet instantly."

Many feel that chip implants will become as common as contact lenses in the not-too-distant future.

Let me remind you that the false prophet *"causes all, both small and great, rich and poor, free and slave, to receive a mark on their right hand or on their foreheads"* (Revelation 13:16). The "mark" is not just this chip, but could certainly be part of it.

ISLAMIC PRAYERS AT THE VATICAN

The last week of May, 2014, Pope Francis flew to Jordan and Israel. He became the first pontiff to go into the West Bank. At Bethlehem, he took the unprecedented step of referring to the Israeli-occupied territory as the "State of Palestine."

Then, in Jerusalem, he visited the Muslim-controlled Dome of the Rock. There, speaking to Muslim leaders, he addressed listeners as "'brothers'— rather than 'friends,' as indicated in his prepared text (Catholic News Service, May 26, 2014).

The theme of his remarks to Muslims, Christians, and Jews during this visit was one of unity, reconciliation, and the importance of becoming "one."

The newsmaker of the journey was the fact that Pope Francis invited representatives from the three dominant religions to join him in Rome for a prayer meeting.

That event took place two weeks later, on Pentecost Sunday, June 6, 2014. Present were Israel president Shimon Perez, Palestinian president Mahmoud Abbas, Argentine Rabbi Abraham Skorka, and Muslim leader Sheik Omar Aboud.

Together, these men read from their scriptures and prayed their prayers. There were no religious symbols visible. Most significant, for the first time in history, Islamic prayers were uttered from the Vatican—in the city of the seven hills.

Let me remind you what we discussed in chapter two, regarding the false prophet bringing the three major religions of the world together under the theme, "Let's unite. We are all praying to the same God."

On September 4, 2014, the *Jewish Daily*

Report carried the news that Shimon Peres, former president of Israel, called for a United Nation of Religions.

THE FALSE PROPHET

Shortly before he died in 1226, Saint Francis of Assisi uttered these prophetic words, "Some preachers will keep silent about the truth, and others will trample it under foot and deny it. Sanctity of life will be held in derision even by those who outwardly profess it, for in those days Jesus Christ will send them not a true Pastor, but a destroyer."

And during the 20th century, the noted Archbishop Fulton Sheen, made this astounding statement:

"The False Prophet will have a religion without a cross. A religion without a world to come. A religion to destroy religions. There will be a counterfeit church. Christ's Church [the Catholic Church] will be one. And the False Prophet will create the other.

The false church will be worldly ecumenical, and global. It will be a loose federation of churches. And religions forming some type of global association. A world parliament of churches. It will be emptied of all divine content and will be the mystical body of the Antichrist. The mystical body on earth today will have its Judas Iscariot and he will be the false prophet. Satan will recruit him from among our bishops."

This brings us full circle to the prophecy of Saint Malachy regarding the final pope—Peter the Roman—will "pasture his sheep through many tribulations and when these things are finished the city of seven hills will be destroyed. And the dreadful Judge will judge his people. The end."

I remind you of the ten horns [nations] that will *"hate the harlot...eat her flesh and burn her with fire"* (Revelation 17:16).

I am deeply concerned for my brothers and sisters in the Lord who have flown to Rome and met with the pope. One by one they return, praising Pope Francis, telling me that he is preaching *"the unity of the faith"* (Ephesians 4:13) so that the fulness of Christ may be established on earth.

That is fine if the unity of the saints is in Christ alone, but not universalism.

To say that Jesus died for everybody and we are all going to heaven (whether we accept Him or not) is a lie. The Bible tells us, *"If you confess with your mouth the Lord Jesus and believe in your heart that God has raised Him from the dead, you will be saved"* (Romans 10:9).

In this hour, we cannot stand hand in hand with anyone who says you can get to heaven by any other means than the blood of Christ and by His grace. Remember, Jesus warns, *"Take heed that no one deceives you. For many will come in My name, saying, 'I am the Christ,' and will deceive many"* (Matthew 24:4-5).

I agree with the humanitarian aspects of Christianity that the poor should be fed, loved, and clothed. We do that in our church, at home and through missions. But we cannot, must not, and *will not* lay down our belief in what Jesus declared: *"I am the way, the truth, and the life. No one comes to the Father except through Me"* (John 14:6).

We are not all on paths that lead to utopia. I pray that Muslims come to the light of the Gospel, accept Jesus Christ, and have eternal life with Him.

In light of the rise of radical Islam, our government does not seem to understand that when people are so mentally deranged that they would march innocent children in front of rockets to become shelters for incoming bombs, that's demonic. You cannot negotiate with such unhinged minds. I believe the only hope they have is to have those demons cast out and the glorious Spirit of the Lord Jesus Christ enter their hearts and rebirth their lost and depraved lives.

THE PEACE PROCESS

People ask me, "Aren't you for peace in the Middle East?"

I certainly am, but I have also read my Bible that tells me there will be no peace until the Prince of Peace returns. Specifically, Scripture states, *"...the day of the Lord so comes as a thief in the night. For when they say, 'Peace and safety!' then sudden destruction comes upon them"* (1 Thessalonians 5:2-3).

Major Christian leaders may continue to go down the path of unity and universalism, but if they mislead the bride, the body of Christ, God will remove them. Jesus didn't die on the cross for man to rob the Gospel of the truth.

Thank God there is a remnant—an outpouring of the Holy Spirit—in Latin America, Africa, America, and many nations. Jesus said, *"And this gospel of the kingdom will be preached in all the world as a witness, and then the end will come"* (Matthew 24:14).

Every believer needs to be awake to the signs of the times and aware of the rise of the false prophet.

Now, let's look at the who, what, where, and when of the Antichrist.

PART TWO

THE ANTICHRIST

CHAPTER 5

THE SWEET AND BITTER BOOK

One of the undeniable truths of Scripture is that the rapture of the church will take place. It is not a myth or a fable. According to 1 Thessalonians 4:16-17, *"For the Lord Himself will descend from heaven with a shout, with the voice of an archangel, and with the trumpet of God. And the dead in Christ will rise first. Then we who are alive and remain shall be caught up together with them in the clouds to meet the Lord in the air. And thus we shall always be with the Lord."*

The question that has been debated for centuries regards *when* the rapture will occur.

I am often asked, "Are you a pre-tribulation, mid-tribulation, or a post-tribulation person?"

As I will detail in this chapter, I believe the

rapture will happen pre-tribulation.

Many who hold the "mid" and "post" position, like to quote Revelation 10:7, *"In the days of the sounding of the seventh angel, when he is about to sound, the mystery of God would be finished, as He declared to His servants the prophets."*

They believe the rapture will take place when *"the mystery of God would be finished"*; therefore, it must be at the end of the Tribulation.

But within that same verse is the key to what John was speaking of in his revelation. The mystery would conclude *"as He declared to His servants the prophets."*

THE CULMINATION OF THE AGES

Biblical scholars have determined that the apostle wrote this between 95 and 100 AD. So he is referring to only the writings of the prophets he had access to—the Old Testament prophets from Isaiah to Malachi. And he is specifically referencing the prophets he had read pertaining to the coming of the Messiah. Now, in this moment, the culmination of the ages and purposes, for all of Scripture, is about to be fulfilled. In other words, what the prophets foretold was nearing completion.

Some are of the opinion that *"the sounding of the seventh angel"* in verse 7 is the sound of the trumpet at the rapture. But it is not.

It is the seventh angel blowing a seventh trumpet of judgment at the midway point of the 70th week of Daniel, of the seven year Tribulation. This is 42 months (or three-and-a-half years) in. To be more specific, it is the signal of the beginning of the Great Tribulation.

The reason I know this is true is because of what takes place next, as John writes in the verse that follows: *"Then the voice which I heard from heaven spoke to me again and said, 'Go, take the little book which is open in the hand of the angel who stands on the sea and on the earth'"* (Revelation 10:8).

I believe "the earth" in this verse speaks specifically of the Middle East.

Next, John writes, *"So I went to the angel and said to him, 'Give me the little book.' And he said to me, 'Take and eat it; and it will make your stomach bitter, but it will be as sweet as honey in your mouth.' Then I took the little book out of the angel's hand and ate it, and it was as sweet as honey in my mouth. But when I had eaten it, my stomach became bitter. And he said to me, 'You must prophesy again about many peoples, nations, tongues, and kings'"* (verses 9:11).

IDENTIFYING THE BOOK

Here is the question: What little book did John devour?

He is eating a book containing the mystery that Almighty God has revealed to the prophets (Isaiah to Maliachi). It is the Book of Daniel.

Please pay close attention to Daniel 12:1: *"At that time Michael shall stand up the great prince who stands watch over the sons of your people [Israel]. And there shall be a time of trouble, such as never was..."*

As confirmed in the same chapter, Daniel is speaking of the last three-and-a-half years of the Tribulation. Remember, Jesus said that even during the Great Tribulation there would be deliverance for the elect (see Matthew 24:21-22). This is a reference to Israel.

Daniel continued writing, *"At that time your*

people shall be delivered, every one who is found written in the book. And many of those who sleep in the dust of the earth shall awake, some to everlasting life, some to shame and everlasting contempt. Those who are wise shall shine like the brightness of the firmament, and those who turn many to righteousness like the stars forever and ever " (Daniel 12:1-3).

Let me encourage you to underline the next verse in your Bible: *"But you Daniel, shut up the words and seal the book until the time of the end. "* What time is God pointing to? When *"many shall run to and fro, and knowledge shall increase"* (verse 4).

The prophet adds, *"Then I, Daniel, looked; and there stood two others, one on this riverbank and the other on that riverbank. And one said to the man clothed in linen, who was above the waters of the river, 'How long shall the fulfillment of these wonders be?'"* (verses 5-6).

THE TIME LINE

If you want to know when the mystery is

unveiled and the trumpet blast echoes through the sky, pay attention to the answer Daniel received: *"Then I heard the man clothed in linen, who was above the waters of the river, when he held up his right hand and his left hand to heaven, and swore by Him who lives forever, that it shall be for a time, times, and half a time..."* (verse 7).

Time is one year, *times* is two years, and *half a time* is six months; that's three-and-a-half years (42 months or 1,260 days, according to the Hebrew calendar).

God is revealing through Daniel that the book is sealed until the half way point—the release of the Great Tribulation.

Daniel was also told: *"...when the power of the holy people has been completely shattered, all these things shall be finished."* (verse 7). Then he writes, *"Although I heard, I did not understand. Then I said [to the angel], 'My lord, what shall be the end of these things?" And he said, 'Go your way, Daniel, for the words are closed up and sealed till the time of the end'"* (verses 8-9).

It is my opinion, and that of many others, that John ate the 12-chapter Book of Daniel—the little book that he was commanded to consume by the seventh angel with the seventh trumpet (Revelation 10).

The reason he could say that the book was "*as sweet as honey in my mouth*" (verse 10) is because he saw the coming of the Messiah and the restoration of the kingdom of God. At the same time, however, it was "*bitter in his stomach*" since he also witnessed an enemy rising up against Zion—Israel, God's people. This would usher in a time of trouble such as the world had never known.

THE ABOMINATION OF DESOLATION

Immediately after eating the Book of Daniel, John was given further instructions, which are recorded in Revelation 11.

The angel handed John a yardstick and told him: "*Rise and measure the temple of God, the altar, and those who worship there. But leave out the court which is outside the temple, and do not measure it, for it has been given to the Gentiles. And they will tread the holy city underfoot for forty-two months"* (verses 1-2).

This speaks of the three-and-a-half years into the Tribulation when the time of the Gentiles shall be fulfilled. These are the people who are led by the Antichrist, who arrives at the moment of the "abomination of desolation," to take the Jews out of the temple and establish himself as god.

This was made known to Daniel by the angel who spoke of *"the time that the daily sacrifice is taken away, and the abomination of desolation is set up"* (Daniel 11:31).

Jesus also warned, *"Therefore when you see the 'abomination of desolation,' spoken of by Daniel the prophet, standing in the holy place (whoever reads, let him understand), then let those who are in Judea flee to the mountains"* (Matthew 24:15-16).

This means the House of God is made bare by a despicable act—when the Antichrist walks into the temple and removes the sacrifice of the Jewish people from the altar and declares that he, and he alone, is divine and must be worshiped.

This is the hour when the false prophet announces that the whole world must worship the Antichrist as god. The Bible declares, *"He causes all, both small and great, rich and poor, free and slave, to receive a mark on their right hand or on their foreheads, and that no one may buy or sell except one who has the mark or the name of the beast, or the number of his name"* (Revelation 13:15-17).

All of mankind will fawn after and bow before this man who has brought a false peace. The city of Jerusalem will be his headquarters during the last 42 months (three-and-a-half years) of this seven year period.

The dragon (the devil himself) working through the Antichrist and the false prophet will form an unholy trinity that will operate a kingdom of darkness from the center of Jerusalem.

THE TWO WITNESSES

It is in this season that the "two witnesses" (spoken of in Revelation 11) arrive on the scene.

Many place the time line of the two witnesses (I believe wrongly) at the end of the Tribulation.

According to Scripture, the two witnesses come back from the Old Testament. They preach and prophesy that Yeshua is the HaMashiach (My Salvation)—the Messiah.

The reason this event does not take place at the end of the Tribulation is because at that late date their message would have no effect. They appear in the middle of the Tribulation so that the whole world will be aware of and see these two men.

There is much guesswork and speculation as to who these individuals are. Some say they are Moses and Elijah, but I think they are Enoch and Elijah, because neither of them had tasted the sting of death. They were both carried up into the heavens while they were still alive (see Hebrews 11:5 and 2 Kings 2:11).

SEEN BY THE WORLD?

I remember as a young boy when my father would preach on this topic and people would question, "It's impossible for the whole world to see the two witnesses!"

Then came satellite television and the doubters changed their tune. Now they were exclaiming, "These really *are* the last days. Prophecy is truly being played out before our eyes."

What is the result of the two witnesses delivering their message to the four corners of the earth? According to Scripture, *"When they finish their testimony, the beast that ascends out of the bottomless pit will make war against them, overcome them, and kill them. And their dead bodies will lie in the street of the great city...where also our Lord was crucified"* (Revelation 11:7-8).

The Bible goes on to describe how people from *"tribes, tongues, and nations will see their dead bodies"* fallen in the streets for three-and-a-half days and rejoice over them, *"because these two prophets tormented those who dwell on the earth"* (verses 9-10).

But this is not the end of the story. John saw how *"after the three-and-a-half days the breath of life from God entered them, and they stood on their feet, and great fear fell on those who saw them"* (verse 11).

Next, there was a loud voice from above calling to the two witnesses, "Come up here!" And they *"ascended to heaven in a cloud"* (verse 12).

That same hour there was a mighty earthquake and thousands were killed (verse 13).

It is at that moment the seventh trumpet will be heard (verse 16), declaring that the Great Tribulation has begun (that last three-and-a-half years).

It is in this context that the Bible says the "mystery of God" (as declared to the prophet Daniel) will finally come to an end.

Next, we will examine how that happens.

CHAPTER 6

UNVEILING THE MYSTERY

Long before my time, students of Scripture, Bible scholars, and prophecy teachers began their search to understand the "mystery" Daniel received and how it relates to what is spoken of in Revelation.

To unravel the secret, let's begin with what God revealed to Daniel. In a vision, he saw four beasts rising out of the sea:

1. A Lion

"The first was like a lion, and had eagle's wings. I watched till its wings were plucked off; and it was lifted up from the earth and made to stand on two feet like a man, and a man's heart was given to it" (Daniel 7:4).

2. A Bear

"And suddenly another beast, a second, like a bear. It was raised up on one side, and had three ribs in its mouth between its teeth. And they said thus to it: 'Arise, devour much flesh!'" (verse 5).

3. A Leopard

"After this I looked, and there was another, like a leopard, which had on its back four wings of a bird. The beast also had four heads, and dominion was given to it" (verse 6).

4. The Unnamed Beast

"After this I saw in the night visions, and behold, a fourth beast, dreadful and terrible, exceedingly strong. It had huge iron teeth; it was devouring, breaking in pieces, and trampling the residue with its feet. It was different from all the beasts that were before it, and it had ten horns. I was considering the horns, and there was another horn, a little one, coming up among them, before whom three of the first horns were plucked out by the roots. And there, in this horn, were eyes like the eyes of a man, and a mouth speaking pompous words" (verses 7-8).

DESCRIPTION OF THE FOURTH BEAST

The prophet was not allowed to share who this fourth beast was, because God ordered: *"Daniel, shut up the words, and seal the book until the time of the end"* (Daniel 12:4).

Jumping ahead to Revelation 10, John eats the Book of Daniel—and immediately after he did, the two witnesses appear, followed by the sound of the seventh trumpet (chapter 11).

The "mystery" is revealed in Revelation 13, when God makes known to John what Daniel was forbidden to disclose.

This brings us to the question: Who is this fourth beast?

Our discovery begins with the words of John: *"Then I stood on the sand of the sea. And I saw a beast rising up out of the sea, having seven heads and ten horns, and on his horns ten crowns, and on his heads a blasphemous name"* (Revelation 13:1).

As we will see, the seven heads represented seven kingdoms: five *were* already established, one *was*, at the time of John, and one *will be* at some point in the future.

The ten horns speak of a coalition of nations that will receive their authority from the Antichrist.

Then John describes the beast—as a leopard, a bear, a lion, and one that was unnamed. However, he gave this description: *"The dragon [Satan] gave him his power, his throne, and great authority. And I saw one of his heads as if it had been mortally wounded, and his deadly wound was healed. And all the world marveled and followed the beast. So they worshiped the dragon who gave authority to the beast; and they worshiped the beast, saying, 'Who is like the beast? Who is able to make war with him?'"* (verses 2-4).

Where did John the apostle receive this information? It came straight from God, as he ate the Book of Daniel. Remember, Daniel spoke of four beasts rising out of the sea; *"like a lion"* (Daniel 7:3), *"like a bear"* (verse 5), *"like a leopard"* (verse 6), and the fourth an unnamed beast (verses 7-8).

Later, in John's revelation, we learn that the fourth beast appears at the midway point of the Tribulation: *"And he was given a mouth speaking great things and blasphemies, and he was given authority to continue for forty-two months.* (Revelation 13:5).

When he appears to die, and is *"mortally wounded"* (verse 3) in one of his heads before being healed, I do not believe this refers to a physical wound. Rather, to one of the nations under the false prophet, it will look as if he has "lost it" mentally.

God also revealed to John: *"The beast that you saw was, and is not, and will ascend out of the bottomless pit and to perdition. And those who dwell on the earth will marvel...when they see the beast that was, and is not, and yet is"* (Revelation 17:8).

This pertains to the Antichrist halfway through the Tribulation—described as the "abomination of desolation." The words in the above verse mentioning *"the beast that was"* means something happened to him.

In past years, I have heard preachers of prophecy interpret this by saying, "The Antichrist will appear to have a gunshot wound in the head and the false prophet would raise him from the dead."

91

However, I believe that his wound was political not physical.

One of the nations that he will lead from will fall, but "the beast" will cause the nations of the earth to rally around this man and resurrect him as a world leader.

He will not just be demonized, he will be demon possessed.

Satan will enter into his body. It is similar to the role Judas played in the earthly ministry of Jesus.

So, politically, the Antichrist makes a comeback. In reading Revelation 13:3, *"...and I saw one of his heads as if it had been mortally wounded"* —remember, the head represents a kingdom or a nation. But then, *"his deadly wound was healed."* Seeing he could pull off such a feat, *"...all the world marveled and followed the beast"* (verse 3).

As we discussed, the false prophet, a major religious leader, will resurrect this nation with his influence, power, and money. The world will see that what was predicted to be an economic, social, and political collapse has been resolved by this man.

It is just one reason why *"All who dwell on the earth will worship him"* (verse 8).

The authority given to this so-called leader is unequaled. *"He opened his mouth in blasphemy against God, to blaspheme His name, His tabernacle, and those who dwell in heaven. It was granted to him to make war with the saints and to overcome them"* (verse 6).

AMAZING COMPARISONS

In studying the prophetic implications of the Antichrist down through the years I have read many texts on the subject. One book in particular that I consider a "must read" is *Unleashing the Beast* by my friend Perry Stone.

Regarding the comparison between Daniel and Revelation, Stone states, "The prophet Daniel and the apostle John lived more than six hundred years apart. Yet, when comparing their visions, it is amazing how the Book of Daniel complements the Book of Revelation. Revelation is a culmination of, and includes deeper explanation of, the apocalyptic visions found in Daniel."

Then Perry Stone notes these parallels:

1. Both saw a final period of seven years.
   Daniel identified the time frame as one
   prophetic week (seven years) in Daniel
   9:27. John divided the seven years into
   two forty-two-month periods (Revelation
   11:2; 13:5).

2. Both saw forty-two final months of world
   history. Daniel gave the time frame as
   time (one year), times (two years), and
   dividing of time (half of a year) (Daniel
   12:7). John said the final time frame
   would be 1,260 days—three and a half
   years (Revelation 12:6).

3. Both identified the Antichrist as a "beast."
   Daniel saw him as the fourth beast that
   would rise to power (Daniel 7:7). John saw
   the Antichrist as the beast rising up from
   the sea (Revelation 13:1).

4. Both reveal a period of great trouble on
   earth. Daniel said it was a time such as
   never was or ever shall be (Daniel 12:1).
   John described a time of wrath and
   trouble (Revelation 12:7-12).

5. Both prophets saw the archangel Michael. Daniel saw Michael standing up at the time of trouble (Daniel 12:1). John saw Michael warring with Satan in heaven (Revelation 12:7).

6. Both prophets saw ten kings that would arise at the end of days. Daniel said the ten horns were ten kings (Daniel 7:24). John saw ten horns with ten crowns that were ten kings (Revelation 13:1).

7. Both saw the resurrection of the dead. Daniel recorded a resurrection after the Tribulation (Daniel 12:2). John saw a resurrection of those who were beheaded in the Tribulation (Revelation 7:9-17).

8. Both prophets saw the return of the Lord to set up His kingdom. Daniel saw an everlasting kingdom of the Messiah (Daniel 7:13-14). John saw Christ returning to make war (Revelation 19:11).

A SIGNIFICANT MATTER

If Daniel had received the mystery of the beasts and could not tell us who the fourth one was, and John saw the beast and *could* reveal him, we'd better pay attention.

Here is why it is imperative to know who the Antichrist is:

- Moses is mentioned in the Bible 768 times.
- Abraham is mentioned 303 times.
- The Messiah is mentioned more than those two giants of the Old Testament put together.
- But the fourth most mentioned person in Scripture is the Antichrist.

To me, this is quite significant.

At this point, I want to remove some erroneous prophetic teaching. There are scores of out-of-print books that predicted the Antichrist was Hitler, Mussolini, Stalin, and a host of world leaders of the past. Some identified United States presidents —including Ronald Regan, Bill Clinton,

George W. Bush, and even Barack Hussein Obama.

Several have written that the Antichrist is a Jew from the tribe of Dan. They use scriptures such as Genesis 49:17: *"Dan shall be a serpent by the way, a viper by the path, that bites the horse's heels so that its rider shall fall backward."* And Jeremiah 8:16: *"The snorting of His horses was heard from Dan. The whole land trembled at the sound of the neighing of His strong ones; for they have come and devoured the land and all that is in it, the city and those who dwell in it."*

They tie this to Revelation 7 that when the tribes of Israel are listed, the absence of Dan means something has happened to that tribe. Therefore, they conclude that because the Old Testament infers that Dan would be no more, out of Dan would come the Antichrist—because the "beast" would need to have influence over Israel.

This is wrong because the Antichrist will not be a Jew.

We need to understand that the reason Dan is missing from the written register is because Dan represents a type of Jew who does not keep the commandments. He is a secular Jew, not one who is religious.

There is what is called a "Sebastian Jew"— named after Mahial Sebastian, an influential Romanian writer living during World War II. He was born to Jewish parents but never baptized into Judaism. Basically, he was a secularist.

Today, Sebastian Jews make up an extremely influential segment of Europe and across the western world. While they may consider themselves Jewish, many are total atheists.

THE GENTILE FACTOR

I believe the Bible places non-religious Jews into the tribe of Dan because, in truth, it would become non-existent. *Believing* Jews are those individuals who have kept the commandments (Revelation 12: 17)—those who teach the Torah, who observe the feasts, and are looking for the Messiah to return.

Here is another logical reason why the Antichrist will not be a Jew. In order to console the world, and especially the Middle East, he would have to convince 1.4 billion Muslims to follow him. No Jew has that kind of influence. In case you hadn't noticed, Islam continually boasts about their aim to annihilate Israel and drive her into the sea.

Perhaps the most convincing reason why the Antichrist will not be Jewish is because all of the kingdoms listed in Daniel 2 are Gentile empires. We know this because Jesus said concerning the last earthly empire: *"For there will be great distress in the land and wrath upon this people. And they will fall by the edge of the sword, and be led away captive into all nations. And Jerusalem will be trampled by Gentiles until the times of the Gentiles are fulfilled"* (Luke 21:23-24).

Remember, Revelation 11:2 mentions that the outer court of the temple *"has been given to the Gentiles. And they will tread the holy city underfoot for forty-two months."*

SACRED OR SYMBOLIC?

Some have questioned whether the Book of Revelation is prophetic or merely an allegory filled with symbolism.

There is a doctrine called "preterism" that began in the early Catholic church that interprets prophecies of Scripture as occurrences which have already taken place. For example, the Book of Daniel is explained as events that happened in the second century BC, while Revelation is seen as events that took place in the first century AD. Those who hold this view believe that everything was fulfilled with the destruction of Jerusalem in 70 AD.

A similar form of this doctrine has crept into contemporary mainline Christian denominations, and even the Southern Baptist churches under the term "amillennialism." They reject the belief that Jesus will have a literal thousand-year-long physical reign on the earth. While they hold that Jesus will return, they believe the Book of Revelation is primarily allegorical and has no literal meaning to it whatsoever—that the thousand years mentioned in Revelation 20 is a symbolic number, not a literal description. They say the millennium has already begun and is identical with the current church age.

In the Southern Baptist Convention, with

40,000 churches across America, most of the pastors who were trained in SBC seminaries, are "amillennial."

There is another group who embrace "Replacement theology"—a teaching that the Christian church has replaced national Israel regarding the plan, purpose, and promises of God. Therefore, as they preach, many of the promises that God made to Israel must be spiritualized.

This theology, along with preterism, was born out of an anti-semitic spirit that facilitated people (such as Hitler) to destroy the Jewish race. The thinking was, "The Jews have no ultimate purpose, so if they are simply in the way and causing a problem, let's get rid of them."

This was a doctrine that had crept into the church and gave birth to Hitler. Many feel this explains why, at the time, the church responded to the Holocaust with such silence.

Allow me to ask this question: If Almighty God needed to write fiction, why would He place it in His book beside the truth? Replacement theology, preterism, and amillennialism are blights on the Christian world.

Some pastors, trying to be "all things to all

men," attempt to sidestep the issue. One preacher smiled and said, "I'm a pan-millennial—I believe it will all pan out in the end!"

You will not find me in that category. If my earthly life and eternal future is at stake, I want to know what is going to take place.

A FUTURE TEMPLE

I think we would be wise to use a dose of common sense. For example, when a person who believes in the preterist doctrine says that the destruction of Jerusalem (spoken of in Revelation 11:2) happened in 70 AD, we need to take a closer look.

The reason John couldn't be prophesying in 70 AD is because he didn't write this until approximately 95-100 AD. Nor does John go and measure the temple, because there *was* no temple at that time. It had been destroyed totally and completely by the Romans. So, when God told John, *"Rise and measure the temple of God"* (Revelation 11:1), he was writing about a future edifice.

There are many Bible preachers who are of the opinion that one of the ways the Antichrist will entice the Jews to follow him is by rebuilding their temple. Nowhere in Scripture is that theory found. But what *is* recorded in the Bible is that the Antichrist will invade the temple at the three-and-a-half year point, as we detailed earlier. This is when he will set up an image of himself and *"All who dwell in the earth will worship him"* (Revelation 13:8).

As we will see, the Bible gives more than clues as to who the Antichrist will be.

CHAPTER 7

THE ANTICHRIST IDENTIFIED

The Bible ascribes numerous names to the Antichrist, including:

1. "The Little Horn"

"I was considering the horns, and there was another horn, a little one, coming up among them, before whom three of the first horns were plucked out by the roots. And there, in this horn, were eyes like the eyes of a man, and a mouth speaking pompous words" (Daniel 7:8).

2. "The King of Fierce Countenance"

"And in the latter time of their kingdom, when the transgressors have reached their fullness, a king shall arise, having fierce

features, who understands sinister schemes" (Daniel 8:23).

3. "The Prince Who is to Come"

"And after the sixty-two weeks Messiah shall be cut off, but not for Himself; and the people of the prince who is to come shall destroy the city and the sanctuary. The end of it shall be with a flood, and till the end of the war desolations are determined" (Daniel 9:26).

4. "One Who Makes Desolate"

"Then he shall confirm a covenant with many for one week; but in the middle of the week He shall bring an end to sacrifice and offering. And on the wing of abominations shall be one who makes desolate, even until the consummation, which is determined, is poured out on the desolate" (Daniel 9:27).

5. "The Vile Person"

"And in his place shall arise a vile person, to whom they will not give the honor of royalty; but he shall come in peaceably, and seize the kingdom by intrigue" (Daniel 11:2).

6. "The Willful King"

"Then the king shall do according to his own will: he shall exalt and magnify himself above every god, shall speak blasphemies against the God of gods, and shall prosper till the wrath has been accomplished; for what has been determined shall be done" (Daniel 11:36).

7. "The Man of Sin"

"Let no one deceive you by any means; for that Day will not come unless the falling away comes first, and the man of sin is revealed" (2 Thessalonians 2:3).

8. "The Son of Perdition"

He is *"the son of perdition, who opposes and exalts himself above all that is called God"* (2 Thessalonians 2:3-4).

9. "The Lawless One"

"For the mystery of lawlessness is already at work; only He who now restrains will do so

until He is taken out of the way" (2 Thessalonians 2:7).

10. "The Antichrist"

"Who is a liar but he who denies that Jesus is the Christ? He is antichrist who denies the Father and the Son" (1 John 2:22).

11. "The Blasphemer"

"And he was given a mouth speaking great things and blasphemies, and he was given authority to continue for forty-two months" (Revelation 13:5).

12. "The Beast"

"When they finish their testimony, the beast that ascends out of the bottomless pit will make war against them, overcome them, and kill them" (Revelation 11:7).

CAUGHT IN THE MIDDLE

Some have taught that the Antichrist will control the global "common market," but I cannot find that anywhere in Scripture. Instead, he will take charge of a new world order and a new type of government. He will control the oil-rich Gulf states that are primarily Muslim, plus much of Europe and the western world.

The economies of Europe, the Middle East, Africa, and the Americas (North, Central, and South) are headed for ruin and collapse. He will usher in an economic revival for a season, but it will not last very long.

Asia, however, will not participate in his global economy; they do not need his money so they will go their own way. As of December, 2014, the United States owed mainland China $1.24 trillion dollars—and is in debt to Japan by almost the same amount.

Let me emphasize again that the reason the Chinese will bring untold numbers of soldiers into the valley of Meggedo is not to kill the Jews, but to fight the Antichrist—because he has caused the world's economy to crash and now they are on the verge of starving to death. They're determined to destroy him, and the Jews are caught in the middle. To them, that is what the battle of Armageddon is all about.

The Antichrist is a man of peace to those who

follow him, but he is a man of the sword to those who exhibit any opposition.

THE SPIRIT AND THE PERSON

W.E. Vines, in his exhaustive work, *Epository Dictionary of New Testament Words*, points out that the word Antichrist (which is only found in the writings of John), means "one who, assuming the guise of Christ, opposes Christ."

Vines also writes: "What the Apostle says of him so closely resembles what he says of the first beast in Revelation 13, and what the Apostle Paul says of the Man of Sin in 2 Thessalonians 2, that the same person seems to be in view in all these passages, rather than the second beast in Revelation 13, the false prophet; for the latter supports the former in all his Antichristian assumptions."

According to the author, a "false Christ," (Matthew 24:24; Mark 13:22) does not deny the existence of Christ. "He trades upon the expectation of His appearance, affirming that he is the Christ. The Antichrist denies the existence of the true God."

So an impostor doesn't necessarily have to simply be against Jesus, he can pretend to *be* Jesus.

Please note that there is a distinct difference between "Antichrist" and "The Antichrist."

- Antichrist is a spirit.
- The Antichrist is a person.

The antichrist spirit has always been in the world. It showed up at the tower of Babel (Genesis 11) and is alive and well at this very moment. You can find this spirit surfacing in many churches —those who have taken the blood out of the Gospel message and are teaching easy grace, easy belief, and the false promise that everybody is going to heaven.

PLANS AND OBJECTIVES

Let's look at the role of the Antichrist, his methods of operation, and his involvement in the final battle:

First: The Antichrist will form a final earthly empire at the end of the age (Daniel 11).

It will be the last empire as we know it.

Second: The Antichrist will make a peace treaty with Israel for seven years, beginning at the very start of Daniel's seventieth week (Daniel 9:24-27).

I believe that week is marked by the sounding of the trump of God, ushering in the Great Tribulation.

Third: The Antichrist will come with a false peace.

He is a man with a dark, depraved mind, *"Who understands sinister schemes"* (Daniel 8:23). He will deceive the Jews into believing that he really wants peace between them and the Muslim world.

For decades, the world's most powerful negotiators have tried to forge harmony between the Jews and the Palestinians, but have failed every time. This man will accomplish this as he sets up his kingdom in Jerusalem (2 Thessalonians 2:4).

Fourth: The Antichrist will be involved in the final battle of Armageddon.

John wrote, *"I saw three unclean spirits like frogs coming out of the mouth of the dragon, out of the mouth of the beast, and out of the mouth of the false prophet. For they are spirits of demons, performing signs, which go out to the kings of the earth and of the whole world, to gather them to the battle of that great day of God Almighty...And they gathered them together to the place called in Hebrew, Armageddon."* (Revelation 16:13-14,16).

HERE IS HIS NAME

The result of my study of Scripture and being faithful to observe what Jesus spoke of as the *"signs of the times"* (Matthew 16:3), has led me to the conclusion that the Antichrist will be Islam's final leader, their messiah—known as the Twelfth Imam. His name is Muhammed al-Mahdi.

There are more than 200 million Shiite Muslims in the world. Iran has the largest number, about 70 million, while Iraq, Pakistan, and India have over 20 million each. The rest are spread across the globe, with an estimated 300,000 Shiite Muslims living in the United States.

The vast majority of this branch of Islam believe in the appearance of "The Twelfth Imam." In fact, some are positive that he is already on earth.

According to their deep-rooted doctrine, the "Twelvers" (as they are sometimes called) trace the lineage from Mohammed through 12 Imams, ending with al-Mahdi. Then, in the year 872 AD, he went into hiding—or as they call it "occultation"—a state of suspended life. They are convinced his appearance on earth is imminent and that he will reestablish the worldwide governance of Islam, which will rule the nations with their interpretation of justice and peace.

Many have observed the actions of the Ayatollahs (religious/political leaders) of Iran and wondered why they are creating such havoc in the Middle East and beyond. This, however, does not surprise those who understand the "Twelfth Imam" teaching. According to their reading of the Koran, and the history of their sect, there must be world chaos and upheaval before he appears

—and that he will bring Jesus with him as his prophet.

In the beginning, the Islamic Antichrist will be viewed as a man of peace, but in the end he will turn into a raging, ravenous dragon.

He will deny the deity of Jesus Christ. The Koran teaches that Jesus was simply an ordinary man who was a prophet. He will also reject that Jesus is the Son of God—because their holy book says Allah has no children. Furthermore, in the Islamic view, anyone who believes Jesus is divine is an infidel and should have their head severed from their body.

Do I believe that the 12th Imam has existed in a suspended state for the past eleven centuries? Absolutely not. But a man will rise to power, the Ayatollahs will name him the Twelfth Imam, and the Shiite world will go into a state of frenzy. Unquestioned acceptance of this individual has been brainwashed into their DNA.

Eventually, the Islam Antichrist will sit in the temple of God which has been rebuilt, and he will demand that the world worship him (1 Thessalonians 2:4).

The nations may, at first, hail him as a hero, but

he receives his power from the dragon (Satan) and his agenda is to make war with the saints of God (Revelation 13:7).

Those who do not convert to his religion will be beheaded—the Muslim form of execution. We only have to see what has been happening in Syria, Iraq, Libya, and Nigeria to understand the treacherous acts carried out under the banner of Islam.

WHY THE CHAOS?

I am weary of apologists expressing, "Islam is a religion of peace." Of course, I am not implying that all Muslims are evil, but at the core and root of Islam lies a "convert or die" doctrine.

We can spend years and invest billions of dollars negotiating over Iran's development of a nuclear bomb, but the only thing that will appease their leaders is to kill the "infidels" of Israel and the West and claim the spoils of everything we possess.

The critical media and Hollywood celebrities may try to impress on you what a selfish, despicable country America is, but with all our faults, we are still the greatest, most benevolent, loving, Gospel-preaching nation on the face of the earth.

It is extremely important that we understand what is taking place all around us—especially in the Middle East:

- Why did fighting break out in Iraq after we subdued the nation with a military surge and handed it over to what was supposed to be a democratic government?

- Who stirred up the civil war in Syria that has left over 200,000 of its citizens dead, and more than 3 million refugees who have fled to other nations?

- Why does Hamas fire rockets into Israel, and Hesbolah cause such mayhem in Lebanon? From whom do they receive their munitions?

- How could Yemen be declared a "success story" by the U.S. president one month, and be overrun by Iran-backed Islamic terrorists the next?

The reason you can trace most of the turmoil flowing out of the Middle East to Iran (and its proxies in several nations) is because the Shiite Muslims truly believe it is the only thing that will bring back their messiah.

Yes, we are on the verge of what the Bible describes as the final kingdom—and I am convinced the Antichrist, its leader, will be a Muslim. His name is Muhammed al-Mahdi.

PART THREE

THE FINAL KINGDOM

CHAPTER 8

THE SUCCESSION OF EMPIRES

It's amazing how the Bible interprets itself —especially the Book of Revelation. For example, on its pages it raises the question of the false prophet and the Antichrist, then turns around and explains who they are and where they come from.

Let us look again at what the angel told John: *"Why did you marvel? I will tell you the mystery of the woman and of the beast that carries her, which has the seven heads and the ten horns"* (Revelation 11:7).

Then, follow these details. Specifically, it was revealed to the apostle: *"The seven heads are seven mountains on which the woman [the harlot church] sits"* (Revelation 17:9). This is an unmistakable description of Rome, the city of seven hills.

There is only one place on earth that houses a world church headquarters and leader—the Vatican City in Rome.

The "woman" in verse 7 is the harlot church that will lead the campaign to make the Antichrist god on earth. As we have detailed, this harlot church is a worldwide denomination led by a major spiritual and political leader. This "woman" is carried on the back of the beast (the Antichrist).

Together, they are a coalition of church and state. Again, the beast on which this woman sits has seven heads and ten horns.

Let me emphasize once more that I hold no ill will toward Catholics. There are many who embrace their liturgy and teaching who are truly saved and love Jesus as their Lord and Savior. But it is the global influence of the Vatican that Satan and the Antichrist are courting and pursuing. And they will seize it during the Tribulation.

Now let's focus on Revelation 7:10: *"There are also seven kings. Five have fallen, one is, and the other has not yet come."*

During John's day, there had been five kingdoms (or worldwide empires):

1. Egypt—during the time of the Pharaohs.
2. Syria—ancient Assyria.
3. Babylon—where Daniel and the Jews were in exile.
4. The Medo-Persian Empire—under the rule of Cyrus and Darius.
5. Greece—led by Alexander the Great.

These five kingdoms had collapsed, so when John wrote, *"Five have fallen, [and] one is"* —he was speaking of Rome, which was the empire that had conquered the territories and was in charge at the time of his exile on the Isle of Patmos.

But what about *"the other [which] has not yet come. And when he comes, he must continue a short time"* (verse 10)? To me, and a host of other students of prophecy, this refers to the Western coalition of nations that exists today.

Around our planet, when there are decisions made concerning wars, famine, and atrocities, where do the suppressed and needy look for help? They turn to the "seventh empire"—the United States of America and the European Union. Our nation is 200-plus years old, and Europe has been around longer but has grown in influence with the "EU."

So, as far as time is concerned, we are relatively young—and we fit the description of an empire that will exist for just a short period.

THE EIGHTH KINGDOM

Bible prophecy teachers of the past have been off track when they proposed that the Antichrist will emanate from this American-European coalition. I must admit that several years ago I believed that the Antichrist would arise from the Western division of the revived Roman Empire.

However, many had forgotten that this empire stood on two legs—the East division and a West division. It seemed that all we zeroed in on was the Western branch—the one we as Americans came out of.

Nevertheless, the Eastern division was centered in Constantinople (now in Islam-controlled Turkey) and was home to some of the greatest Christian churches in the world. There was a major split of the Eastern church (Orthodox) and the Western church (Catholic), but the Roman Empire and its political power was established on those two legs.

The Bible speaks of *"The beast that was, and is not, is himself also the eighth, and is of the seven"* (Revelation 17:11).

In other words, the Antichrist surfaces from the seventh kingdom and becomes the eighth. This lines up with the "beast" being a Muslim, arising from what was formerly the Eastern branch of the Roman Empire.

If we look at the five kingdoms listed above and see which has fallen, we can conclude from which nation the Antichrist will emerge and lead.

The reason the Western division is not the kingdom of the Antichrist, is because that's where the false prophet and the false church will spring up from—Rome.

Look for a moment at the Eastern division. Primarily it was comprised of Egypt, Syria, Iran, Greece, and Rome (where the East branch originated).

Let us examine those empires as they stand today:

- Egypt still exists
- Syria still exists

- Iran still exsits
- Greece still exists—and so does Rome.

The nation that does not stand on its own at the present time is Babylon—modern day Iraq.

When we stop to think about the world situation, Americans have grown weary of dealing with Iraq and Afghanistan where many of our brave soldiers gave their lives for a cause that we as a nation have yet to figure out. Much blood was shed for a country that has not been rebuilt.

My personal opinion is that it is impossible to support or reorganize a government that is controlled by demonized leaders who think they are obeying the orders of a god of vengeance, not a God of love.

The current state of affairs remains volatile and tragic—with untold numbers of Christians being killed because they are considered infidels by the Islamic terrorists rampaging through that part of the world.

May God protect America from what is happening in these Muslim countries. If this barbarism ever reached our shores, we would quickly find out who the true Christians are.

If an Islamic jihadist held your child by the throat and demanded, "You either renounce Jesus or I'm going to cut your baby's head off!"—what would be your response?

OH, BABYLON

I believe Iraq is where the kingdom of the Antichrist will be established for the first three-and-a-half years.

If you remember, Sadam Hussein believed that if he rebuilt the ancient city of Babylon he would become the global leader. He had the spirit of Antichrist on him.

Why is Babylon so significant? It is where the *first* spirit of Antichrist showed up on the earth in the person of Nimrod—the great-grandson of Noah who was the leader of those who built the Tower of Babel in the land of Shinar. God was so displeased at their attempt to erect a tower reaching to the heavens that He confused their languages and *"scattered them abroad over the face of all the earth"* (Genesis 11:9).

Babylon is also the place where the Jewish nation spent 70 years in captivity (Jeremiah 29).

In New Testament days, the Christian church had spread as far as that land (1 Peter 5:13). Those were the believers who the Apostle Peter was addressing when he wrote: *"Beloved, do not think it strange concerning the fiery trial which is to try you, as though some strange thing happened to you; but rejoice to the extent that you partake of Christ's sufferings, that when His glory is revealed, you may also be glad with exceeding joy"* (1 Peter 4:13).

Babylon is mentioned 12 times in the New Testament—and we learn that there is both a physical and a spiritual Babylon. This city is ancient Shinar, where the Bible prophesied that from that place a scroll containing a curse and a woman named "Wickedness" would manifest herself (Zechariah 5:1-11).

Research by Perry Stone uncovered this quote in the 1940 edition of *The Annotated Bible* by Bible scholar Finas Dake: "One thing is certain —Babylon will be the center of activities in the East during the last days in commerce, religion, and politics. It will be rebuilt and become the capital of the Antichrist. He will come from Syria, which will take in Babylon in those days, for the

Syrian division of the old Grecian empire included all the countries of Syria and Iraq."

THE ISRAELI-PALESTINIAN CONFLICT

It should be no surprise to us why Babylon is the place from which the spirit of the Antichrist springs. When God cast Lucifer out of heaven (Isaiah 14:12-15), he was thrown down into the middle of Iraq—where the ancient Garden of Eden was located.

Then God prophesied concerning Syria; that He would *"break the Assyrian in My land, and on My mountains tread him underfoot"* (verse 25).

This reads like today's media headlines!

Even more, the Almighty said concerning ancient Philistia (modern day Gaza): *"Do not rejoice, all you of Philistia, because the rod that struck you is broken; for out of the serpent's roots will come forth a viper, and its offspring will be a fiery flying serpent"* (verse 29).

But during the Tribulation something even worse will occur. From the viper and flying serpent that will come out of Satan—the Antichrist will emerge from Babylon. He will pursue Jerusalem as his headquarters. But the people who have been attacked by Israel should not rejoice when Jerusalem is overrun, because the end is not yet.

I am convinced this is a direct reference to the Israeli-Palestinian conflict—between this woman called Israel (in Revelation 12) and Satan, the fiery red dragon himself.

The reason there will not be peace in the Middle East between the Palestinians and the Jews is due to the turmoil Iran will continue to create in order to set the stage for their so-called "Twelfth Imam" to appear—the Antichrist.

As you read this, we are hurdling toward these cataclysmic events.

CHAPTER 9

THE APOCALYPTIC AGENDA

It is impossible to over-emphasize the mindset of Shiite Islamic religious leaders regarding who I have identified in this book as the Antichrist —"The Twelfth Imam," Muhammed al-Mahdi.

His expected arrival affects not only their spiritual decisions, but their political and military actions. That's what most in the media totally overlook when they see Iran stirring up trouble. Again, Shiites believe it is conflict and chaos that will bring back their "savior"—so the more disruptions they can cause, the better.

Many remember the war between Iraq and Iran that lasted from 1980 to 1988. Sadam Hussein was a Sunni Muslim, fighting against Shiite Muslim Iran, despite the fact that Iraq was and still is a Shiite-majority nation (nearly 70 percent of the population).

Iraq, the land of Babylon, is where several Islamic clerics declare they have spoken directly to the spirit of Muhammed al-Mahdi. Millions actually believe he has been hiding in a cave near the border of Iraq and Syria for hundreds of years. These clerics keep the hopes of the faithful alive by announcing, "I have spoken to him. He is alive!"

Others, in Syria, Lebanon, Iraq, and Iran claim that the spirit of the Twelfth Imam makes appearances in Muslim worship services.

It is essential to focus on *where* the Antichrist will come from, so when we look at what is taking place all around us, we can see how the pieces of the prophetic puzzle are falling into place. The picture becomes more and more clear.

ON SCHEDULE

Leading up to the arrival of the Antichrist, there are several factors that must line up. They involve geography, politics, and fit into a schedule that has been foretold since the days of the prophets.

It is difficult for us to think in terms of eternity—time with no end, yet the Lord does speak of certain times and specific seasons. For example, concerning the return of Christ, Scripture says, *"the Son of Man is coming at an hour you do not expect"* (Matthew 24:44).

There is also a schedule regarding events of the last days and the Tribulation. For instance, leading up to Armageddon, the Bible tells us that in "one hour" kings will receive their power to rule. As God told John the Apostle, *"The ten horns which thou sawest are ten kings, which have received no kingdom as yet; but receive power as kings one hour with the beast"* (Revelation 17:12 KJV).

However, don't look at the term "one hour" as necessarily a 60-minute period. It is best translated as "an appointed time."

There is an agenda that will take place during the Tribulation that impacts the nations.

In Daniel 7 (which also speaks of the beast with ten horns) we are told that *"the four winds of heaven were stirring up the Great Sea"* (verse 2).

The sea referred to in this verse is the Mediterranean. The shores of its waters link (among other nations) Israel, Greece, Turkey, Italy, Spain, and North Africa.

THE "LITTLE HORN"

It is interesting to read the writings of one of the early church fathers, Hippolytus of Rome (170 –236 AD). As the most prominent Christian theologian of his day, here's how he interpreted the four beasts of Daniel 7:

- The lion was ancient Babylon.
- The bear was the Meads and Persians (modern day Iran).
- The leopard was Greece (Alexander the Great's kingdom).
- The fourth (unnamed beast) was Rome.

Daniel, after prophesying that the kingdom of Antichrist will be like all of these kingdoms combined, described the fourth beast as being *"dreadful and terrible, exceedingly strong. It had huge iron teeth; it was devouring, breaking into pieces, and trampling the residue with its feet"* (Daniel 7:7).

Then, as he was examining the ten horns of this beast, he noticed *"another horn, a little one, coming up among them"* (verse 8). In other words, the "little horn" will rise after the ten horns have been established.

As this applies to the end of days, there is a ten nation coalition which will be formed by the midpoint of the Tribulation—and a smaller nation will emerge out of them.

THREE FALLEN NATIONS

As God continued His revelation to Daniel, out of one of the horns *"came a little horn which grew exceedingly great toward the south, toward the east, and toward the Glorious Land [Israel]"* (Daniel 9:9). This territory will be the kingdom of the Antichrist.

Daniel also mentions that the little horn grows to such power that it will overthrow three kingdoms and bring them into its possession:

"At the time of the end the king of the South shall attack him; and the king of the North shall come against him like a whirlwind, with chariots, horsemen, and with many ships; and he shall enter the countries,

overwhelm them, and pass through.

He shall also enter the Glorious Land, and many countries shall be overthrown... He shall stretch out his hand against the countries, and the land of Egypt shall not escape.

He shall have power over the treasures of gold and silver, and over all the precious things of Egypt; also the Libyans and Ethiopians shall follow at his heels" (Daniel 11:40-43).

Scholars of Scripture, going back to the early centuries AD, have agreed that at the end of time those three nations—Egypt, Libya, and Ethiopia—would fall. In the natural, even just a few years ago, that assumption would seem impossible, especially with strong military dictators such as Hosni Mubarak in Egypt and Muammar Gaddafi in Libya.

Then, in 2011, came the "Arab Spring"—which turned out to be an Islamic hurricane. Now, countries like Egypt and Libya are so unstable that they could be taken over by the Antichrist without much more than a snap of his finger.

When we look at the winds of change blowing

over the weak governments of Syria, Yemen, Iraq, Afghanistan and other nations in the Middle East—all under Islamic law—it is easy to see how a powerful Muslim man will rise to power. The kings and leaders of that region will pledge their allegiance to him in that "hour" which was prophesied. He will also become the first Islamic leader to have control of Israel.

Regarding the ten nation coalition of the Antichrist, I believe it begins with 13—Iran, Iraq, Pakistan, Afghanistan, Greece, Macedonia, Syria, Lebanon, Israel, Tunisia, Egypt, Libya, and Ethiopia. Those final three are swallowed up by the Antichrist, leaving ten.

When you look at a map of the region, you almost have to take a magnifying glass to find Israel—a sliver of land about the size of New Jersey. If you travel from Israel's Mediterranean city of Netanya to the Palestinian West Bank town of Tukarim, it is a journey of less than ten miles!

Israel is literally surrounded by Muslim nations, making it a ripe target. It is not difficult to visualize how easy it will be for the powerful Islamic Antichrist to overrun this small country. However, Antichrist is unaware that God has a divine plan to destroy Babylon and ultimately save His chosen people.

THE "HARLOT" DESTROYED

This brings us to the question: What happens to Rome? As we earlier detailed, it is the "harlot church" written of in Scripture.

In the revelation given to John, the angel told him, "*The waters which you saw, where the harlot sits, are peoples, multitudes, nations, and tongues. And the ten horns which you saw on the beast, these will hate the harlot, make her desolate and naked*" (Revelation 17:15-16).

The ten nations Rome has been in covenant with will turn on her. This is because they are Muslim and she appears to be Christian—though we know her actions are false at that time.

What will Islam do to Rome? Scripture graphically describes how they will *"eat her flesh and burn her with fire. For God has put it into their hearts to fulfill His purpose, to be of one mind, and to give their kingdom to the beast, until the words of God are fulfilled. And the woman whom you saw is that great city which reigns over the kings of the earth"* (verses 15-18).

Now you see who is in charge. The Almighty is orchestrating every event to finally destroy the enemy and establish His final, glorious, eternal kingdom.

At the end of this horrendous conflict, the "woman" will be destroyed. During the final battle, when the Antichrist is in control of most of the earth's wealth, he will collapse the economy, and the influence of the "harlot" will be no more.

All of these things must take place in order for the curtain to be pulled back on the greatest moment in human history.

CHAPTER 10

THE KING OF KINGS RIDES IN!

For decades, believers have heard that we are living in the "end times," but prophecy is being fulfilled at such an alarming pace that I truly believe the clock is about to strike midnight!

Today, there are signs in nature (Luke 21:11), in society (2 Timothy 3:1-4), in world politics (Matthew 24:6-7), and in technology (Luke 21:26). But, more than ever, I feel we should pay close attention when the Bible tells us, *"And it shall happen in that day that I will make Jerusalem a very heavy stone for all peoples; all who would heave it away will surely be cut in pieces, though all nations of the earth are gathered against it"* (Zechariah 12:3).

Somehow, this truth is falling on deaf ears.

In a recent Gallup survey, only 25 percent of Americans 29 years old and younger agree that

Israel has the right to defend itself. The vast majority of young adults think Israel is in the wrong.

Evidently, they are being swayed by the media or by liberal university professors. But I have news for them: while other nations will crumble, according to the Bible, Israel will still remain standing.

There is only one conclusion: If you are against Israel, you are against God. That is not simply my opinion, it is written in Scripture:

- **Israel is a chosen nation:**
  "For you [Israel] are a holy people to the Lord your God; the Lord your God has chosen you to be a people for Himself, a special treasure above all the peoples on the face of the earth" (Deuteronomy 7:6).

- **God's covenants are eternal:**
  The Almighty told Abraham: *"I will establish My covenant between Me and you and your descendants after you in their generations, for an everlasting covenant"* (Genesis 17:7).

- **The land was given to Israel permanently:**
  "Also I give to you and your descendants after you...all the land of Canaan, as an everlasting possession" (verse 8).

If your pastor preaches replacement theology and does not stand with the nation of Israel, please find another place to worship. Why? Because that church is under a curse! Again, it's not me saying this, but Almighty God, who declared about Israel, *"I will bless those who bless you, and I will curse him who curses you; and in you all the families of the earth shall be blessed"* (Genesis 12:3).

A SPIRITUAL AWAKENING

One of the signs of the times is that in the last days there is a mighty awakening in the land. For those who have a heart for Israel, love Jesus, and are looking for His return, God's Spirit is being poured out.

Earlier, we mentioned the "spirit of Elijah" (Malachi 4). It will come to fulfill Haggai 2:6-9:

"For thus says the Lord of hosts: 'Once more...I will shake heaven and earth, the sea and dry land; and I will shake all nations, and they shall come to the Desire of All Nations, and I will fill this temple with glory,' says the Lord of hosts. 'The silver is Mine, and the gold is Mine,' says the Lord of hosts. 'The glory of this latter temple shall be greater than the former,' says the Lord of hosts. 'And in this place I will give peace,' says the Lord of hosts."

To the Jews who are looking for the Messiah, God says, *"And it shall come to pass afterward that I will pour out My Spirit on all flesh; your sons and your daughters shall prophesy, your old men shall dream dreams, your young men shall see visions"* (Joel 2:28).

This does not speak of merely a localized revival, but the anointing of the Holy Spirit being poured out all over the earth—bringing new life, supernatural power, and glory upon the house of God.

What does this do for Israel? It awakens them to the fact that the Messiah is soon to appear.

You can travel to Israel today and find Jewish men and women who will say, "You are looking for the Messiah to come the *second* time, but we are looking for Him to arrive the *first* time."

To a Jewish gentleman who told me this, I responded, "Well, if you are looking for Him the first time, and I am looking for Him the second, that means we are talking about the same Messiah."

He just smiled, shrugged his shoulders, and replied, "It's not my time."

Happy Caldwell, founding pastor of the Agape Church in Little Rock, Arkansas, shared with me that during one of his many trips to the Holy Land, his Jewish tour guide stood on the Mount of Olives and talked about the Messiah returning and walking across the Kidron Valley through the Eastern Gate. The guide said, "I am going to run up behind Him and tug on His garment. When He turns around I'm going to ask Him, 'Sir, have You been here before?' And if He replies 'Yes,' I am going to repent and say, 'I'm sorry, I really didn't know it was You.'"

THE TRUE MESSIAH

I am convinced that there are countless Jews who know that Yeshua is the HaMashiach—the true Messiah.

Israeli Prime Minister Netanyahu obviously reads the New Testament. In his speech before the United Nations General Assembly, as reported by the *Washington Post*, October 1, 2013, he called Iranian President Hassan Rouhani, "a wolf in sheep's clothing." This is what Jesus said about false prophets in Matthew 7:15.

Earlier, Netanyahu told an audience in Israel, "Jerusalem is mentioned 142 times in the New Testament" (Reuters News, May 12, 2010).

The Jews are fully aware that both the Old and New Testaments state that they have a right to the territory of Israel. As it is written, *"God promised him [Abraham] that he and his descendants after him would possess the land"* (Acts 7:5). This is why the people of Israel stand firm and declare, "We have a right to be here, and no one will ever force us to leave."

TRIBULATION EVENTS

The Bible is conclusive regarding the events that will take place during the Tribulation. The forces against God are real and will appear to establish a kingdom.

Revelation 17 explicitly states what was written on the forehead of the woman sitting on the scarlet beast: *"MYSTERY, BABYLON THE GREAT, THE MOTHER OF HARLOTS AND OF THE ABOMINATIONS OF THE EARTH"* (verse 5).

The Bible speaks of the *"great city Babylon, that mighty city!"* (Revelation 18:10). It became *"clothed in fine linen, purple and scarlet, and adorned with gold and precious stones and pearls!"* (verse 16).

Babylon is Iraq.

In ancient days, Iraq was much larger than it is now. The territory of the Medo-Persian Empire and the Babylonian Empire included Syria, Iran, Iraq, and much of North Africa.

THE JEWS AND ARMAGEDDON

In the midst of the Antichrist establishing his

kingdom, the Jews—at least 144,000 of them—will be preserved. John saw an angel, carrying the seal of God, cry out, *"Do not harm the earth, the sea, or the trees till we have sealed the servants of our God on their foreheads. And I heard the number of those who were sealed. One hundred and forty-four thousand of all the tribes of the children of Israel were sealed"* (Revelation 7:3-4).

I believe they will be protected and moved to Petra, which is now in Jordan—remaining safe for that final outpouring of the mighty revival that will take place at the end.

The Antichrist will be trying to annihilate God's chosen people who have not taken his own mark—666. Then, at the end of the Tribulation, the preserved Jews will declare that Yeshua is the Messiah.

With drums of war sounding as they approach the final battle, the sixth vial is poured out and the armies of the world converge on Israel. Scripture tells us that *"the spirits of demons...[will] go out to the kings of the earth and of the whole world, to gather them to the battle of that great day of God Almighty"* (Revelation 16:14).

The exact location of this conflict is named:

"And they gathered them together to the place called in Hebrew, Armageddon" (verse 16).

This is the Jezreel Valley, a large fertile plain in northern Israel, between Haifa and Mount Carmel.

What a cataclysmic event! Horses, tanks, and airplanes are everywhere. The whole world is in turmoil as the most devastating earthquakes in human history are shaking the planet (verse 18).

Mountains are collapsing, islands are melting into the sea (verse 20), and demons are being loosed from the bottomless pit.

These, as indicated in Jude, are the demons that cohabited with women and created the giant race of men before the time of Noah. The word "Nephlim" means "fallen ones, giants" and is used to describe the children of a sexual union between *"sons of God"* (fallen angels) and the *"daughters of men"* (Genesis 6:4).

These are *"the angels who did not keep their proper domain, but left their own abode, He has reserved in everlasting chains under darkness for the judgment of the great day"* (Jude 1:6).

Because they were so evil, these demons were designated to a portion of Hell, but now they will be set free on the earth.

John saw men and women pleading to die because of the extreme torment they were suffering. As giant hailstones fell from heaven, *"Men blasphemed God...since that plague was exceedingly great"* (verse 21).

The entire planet is writhing in agony and groaning in despair.

A DEAFENING NOISE

In that moment—and I want you to see this with your spiritual eyes—as it looks like the world will totally collapse, something absolutely incredible takes place.

Just as it seemed that the end of creation was at hand and that Jesus Christ had forgotten everyone, suddenly there came an ear-piercing noise. I want you to hear it!

John writes with emotion and excitement, *"After these things I heard a loud voice of a great multitude in heaven"* (Revelation 19:1).

In the midst of the trembling of Tribulation, an unmistakable sound was heard from above. Who are included in the multitude?

They are the righteous saints of Almighty God

who have been carried away—the bride of Christ—to the Marriage Supper of the Lamb.

Hear them singing and exalting: *"Alleluia! Salvation and glory and honor and power belong to the Lord our God! For true and righteous are His judgments, because He has judged the great harlot who corrupted the earth with her fornication; and He has avenged on her the blood of His servants shed by her"* (verses 1-2).

The saints of God—which includes us—shout for joy, *"Alleluia!"* (verse 3).

As John beautifully describes the scene, *"The twenty-four elders and the four living creatures fell down and worshiped God who sat on the throne, saying, 'Amen! Alleluia!' Then a voice came from the throne, saying, 'Praise our God, all you His servants and those who fear Him, both small and great!'"* (verses 4-5).

Once more, John heard the swell of a huge chorus, *"as the sound of many waters as the sound of mighty thunderings, saying, 'Alleluia! For the Lord God Omnipotent reigns! Let us be glad and rejoice and give Him glory, for the marriage of the Lamb has come, and His wife has made herself ready'"* (verses 6-7).

If you know anything about Jewish wedding traditions of that day, the groom arrives at midnight and sweeps his bride away—taking her into the bridal chamber for seven days.

After the rapture, for seven years the bride will be carried away into the heavens. She will be there for the judgment seat of Christ and for the rewards being handed out. All the saints of God are present.

The bride of Jesus Christ is getting ready, preparing for the Marriage Supper of the Lamb.

In the Jewish wedding, on the seventh day, the groom introduces his bride. She is arrayed in white and appears without spot or wrinkle. He has bathed and adorned his bride—and on that seventh day he proudly presents her at the wedding feast.

For one year, at the end of the Tribulation, we will sit down at the banquet table of our Savior. He will parade you and me—His bride—before the whole world. He has redeemed us by His own blood and we will rejoice at the Marriage Supper of the Lamb.

What a glorious celebration that will be!

SUDDENLY, EVERYTHING CHANGES

At the conclusion of this triumphant year, another major event takes place. While the saints are rejoicing and the earth is in turmoil, God shows John what happens next.

He writes:

"Now I saw heaven opened, and behold, a white horse. And He who sat on him was called Faithful and True, and in righteousness He judges and makes war.

His eyes were like a flame of fire, and on His head were many crowns. He had a name written that no one knew except Himself. He was clothed with a robe dipped in blood, and His name is called The Word of God.

And the armies in heaven, clothed in fine linen, white and clean, followed Him on white horses. Now out of His mouth goes a sharp sword, that with it He should strike the nations. And He Himself will rule them with a rod of iron. He Himself treads the winepress of the fierceness and wrath

of Almighty God.
And He has on His robe and on His thigh
a name written: KING OF KINGS AND
LORD OF LORDS" (Revelation 19:11-16).

Christ is wearing a Jewish robe—a tallit—and the names of God are written on it.

What a moment. Because of pressure from the Antichrist, the Jews are backed in a corner. The armies of China and other nations are in full battle mode. Then Jesus appears, riding in on a white horse, and mankind sees Him in the fullness of the power of His glory. Everything forever changes!

With the fall of Babylon, all that Islam has believed and all that greedy men have hoped for will come crashing down before their very eyes. The Lamb of God, as the Lion of Judah, will enter with a shout and the trump of God.

As believers who have been raised with Christ in the rapture, we will mount the horses with Him and ride back into that Eastern sky.

THE EASTERN GATE

The moment Christ sets His foot down on the

Mount of Olives, the mountain splits in two. The prophecy God gave to Zechariah comes to life: *"Behold, the day of the Lord is coming, and your spoil will be divided in your midst. For I will gather all the nations to battle against Jerusalem...Then the Lord will go forth and fight against those nations, as He fights in the day of battle. And in that day His feet will stand on the Mount of Olives, which faces Jerusalem on the east. And the Mount of Olives shall be split in two, from east to west"* (Zechariah 14:1-4).

Jesus steps down from the horse and walks across the Kidron Valley—through the valley of the shadow of death. Then He triumphantly marches through the Eastern Gate, walks up to the Temple Mount—*"and the Lord God will give Him the throne of His father David...and of His kingdom there will be no end"* (Luke 1:32-33).

Hallelujah!

The Eastern Gate is the same one Christ entered on His way to His crucifixion. It was the gate used to enter Jerusalem from the Mount of Olives.

This gate, which was sealed shut by the Muslims in 1541, is the only one that gives direct access to the Temple Mount. According to Scripture, it will remain shut until Christ returns and is accepted by the Jews.

Remember, Jesus said, *"O Jerusalem, Jerusalem, the one who kills the prophets and stones those who are sent to her! How often I wanted to gather your children together, as a hen gathers her chicks under her wings, but you were not willing! See! Your house is left to you desolate; for I say to you, you shall see Me no more till you say, 'Blessed is He who comes in the name of the Lord!'"* (Matthew 23:37-39).

God gave the prophet Ezekiel this supernatural vision: *"Afterward he brought me to the gate, the gate that faces toward the east. And behold, the glory of the God of Israel came from the way of the east"* (Ezekiel 43:1-2). And he adds, *"The glory of the Lord came into the temple by way of the gate which faces toward the east"* (verse 4).

When Christ returns, the Eastern Gate that was sealed (Ezekiel 44:1-2) will now be opened.

He will rule on that earthly throne for a thousand years—and we will reign with Him (Revelation 20:4-6).

A NEW, ETERNAL KINGDOM

All the souls on earth, whether they be saved or unsaved will be commanded to go to Jerusalem and bow their knee and declare that Jesus Christ is the King of Kings and Lord of Lords.

Paul the Apostle wrote, *"For I do not desire, brethren, that you should be ignorant of this mystery, lest you should be wise in your own opinion, that blindness in part has happened to Israel until the fullness of the Gentiles has come in. And so all Israel will be saved, as it is written: 'The Deliverer will come out of Zion, and He will turn away ungodliness from Jacob; for this is My covenant with them, when I take away their sins"* (Romans 11:25-27).

When the feet of Christ touch the Mount of Olives, all of the Jews who have not accepted Him as Messiah (many hundreds of thousands, if not millions, will have already received Him), will be saved in one day. When they look into the hands of the One whom they pierced, and when they touch His feet and His side, like the doubting disciple Thomas, they will cry, "We are sorry."

Christ will graciously redeem them by His precious blood.

No longer will there be any reason to be concerned with the foes of God. Satan will be *"cast into the lake of fire and brimstone where the beast and the false prophet are. And they will be tormented day and night forever and ever"* (Revelation 20:10).

Peace will fill the earth, and the lion and the lamb will lie down together; a child will play with a viper and not be harmed (see Isaiah 11). The Prince of Peace will rule and reign.

How does it end? *"The kingdoms of this world have become the kingdoms of our Lord and of His Christ, and He shall reign forever and ever!"* (Revelation 11:15).

The apocalypse is rising, but praise God, we who know Christ will rise first, to meet Him in the clouds of glory!